The Loving Dictionary

1,001 Words of Appreciation to Energize, Enrich and Empower All of Your Relationships

by

Marian York

ISBN: 0-7596-5837-4

This book is printed on acid free paper.

1stBooks - rev. 2/1/02

PRAISE FOR THE LOVING DICTIONARY by Marian York

The Loving Dictionary is an awesome, bright and clever resource for all those who care about expanding the amount and quality of love and esteem in this world and dare to do something about it. It is a wonderful resource for developing self-esteem and self-confidence and facilitating the expression of love.
Jack Canfield Speaker, Co-author *Chicken Soup for the Soul* series

What a benevolent, captivating, radical message of hope you have! Thanks for providing a workout of affirmative language that all of us can use in every area of life.
Terry Paulson Psychologist, Author *They Shoot Managers Don't They*

Great book! Great idea! *THE LOVING DICTIONARY* is much needed!
Barbara Sher Speaker, Author *I Could Do Anything If I Only Knew What It Was*

Want to enhance your marriage, personal relationships, and your business alliances? Read *The Loving Dictionary*. Marian York makes it easy to bolster your own self-esteem, while giving other people exactly what they need to excel.
George R. Walther Speaker, Author *Power Talking*

What a great idea! We are so influenced by the words we use daily. This is one book that will be a constant reminder to people to always use words to build instead of destroy.
Wally Amos The Cookie Man *The Power In You*

Wow! What a joyous idea. Truly a people builders dream. *The Loving Dictionary* is for anyone interested in growing oneself or others. Thank you, Marian.
Bob Moawad CEO Edge Learning Institute, Past President National Council for Self Esteem

A wonderful vehicle to help build our confidence and self-esteem through the use of positive reinforcement and affirmations...it's truly empowering! A winner!
Rita Davenport Humorist, Author *Laugh Your Way to Success*

It belongs in every church bookstore and in every family library. I know it will touch and lift others in the same way it touched myself and my family. I'll use it in my pastoral counseling as a tool to help people counter their challenges with a positive focus.
Rob Williams Minister Marble Collegiate Church, New York City

Next to the bible I'll use it more than any other book in our home. *The Loving Dictionary* puts a smile on my face and a valuable source of words at my fingertips. I'll use it daily with my children and look forward to sharing it with our friends.
Nancy Weaver Homemaker, Mother of Ten Fork, Washington

To each and every one of us,

born lovable, capable, beautiful,

intelligent and hopeful

CONTENTS

PREFACE TO THE LOVING DICTIONARY

By Jack Canfield

For the last twenty-one years I have been teaching teachers, managers, parents and spouses how to develop high self-esteem in themselves and others. A core part of this message has always been to focus on the positive, to monitor ones' self talk, and to use the language of affirmation, validation, and empowerment when talking to others.

I teach what I consider to be a basic law of psychology - what I call "The Law of Replacement." This law states that you cannot stop negative, self-defeating self-talk unless you replace it with positive, uplifting and self-empowering self-talk. It doesn't work to just stop the negative verbal patterns. As you probably remember from basic science class, nature abhors a vacuum. If the mental vacuum created by eliminating the negative is not replaced with the positive, it will suck the negative back in.

That's why I love *The Loving Dictionary*. It provides you with a list of positive words to use in describing yourself, to use in creating dynamic and powerful affirmations and to use in describing and affirming those people you love and care about.

Teachers can use this dictionary as a source of positive vocabulary words to teach their students. Parents can use it as a source of positive description for their children. Managers can use it to find words when giving feedback and conducting performance appraisals.

In our book *Chicken Soup for the Soul*,[1] Mark Victor Hansen and I included a story about Sister Helen P. Mrosla, who had her ninth grade students write down "all of the good things" they could think of about each of their classmates. Over the weekend, she then compiled all of the information onto a single sheet of paper for each student.

Seven years later almost every student still had their sheet of paper. Many carried it in their wallets and purses. A student who was killed in Viet Nam was still carrying his list in his wallet when he was shot. This story demonstrates to me how universal and how powerful the need for validation and positive affirmation is. Most of us are literally starved for it. We can start by giving it to ourselves and then sharing it with others. We can become an even more positive force for good in the universe.

---

[1] See *Chicken Soup for the Soul: 101 Stories to Awaken the Heart and Rekindle the Spirit* by Jack Canfield and Mark Victor Hansen. Health Communications 1993, p Beach, Fl.

Words are so powerful that R. Buckminster Fuller, one of the greatest geniuses of our time, stopped using all words for one year and then slowly began speaking again - using only words that would uplift and inspire himself and others.

The Loving Dictionary is an awesome, bright and clever resource for all those who care about expanding the amount and quality of love and esteem in this world and dare to do something about it. It is a wonderful resource for developing self-esteem and self-confidence and facilitating the expression of love and friendship. Make sure you use this valuable resource and use it often. You and those you care about deserve it.

ACKNOWLEDGMENTS

The Loving Dictionary is about appreciation and its very existence is a testament to the power of appreciation. I am very grateful to all the people who have encouraged me at every step of the way. I have never authored a book before, and without their words of appreciation, *The Loving Dictionary* would still be just another great idea.

My heartfelt gratitude goes first and foremost to my long-time friend John Jaeger, the Jaegermeister. His love of words and his belief in this project kept me going as he helped me with the enormous task of selecting and editing the words and their synonyms for the alphabet. I've heard it said that if a book has not been written it's for one of two reasons: either there's no market for it, or it's too hard to do. Without the Jaegermeister's help this book would have been too hard to do.

I extend my joyous thanks to my dear friend Moe Vesey whose simple word game inspired this project and gave me the opportunity to exercise my resourcefulness in ways I had not imagined possible.

With a sigh of relief, I express my appreciation to my editor and book midwife, Shoshana Alexander, whose insight and knowledge helped me take this book through its final stages of birth. She often fed me the very appreciation I was writing about at the times when I most needed the energy to push this project through the birth canal.

I also gratefully acknowledge the many speakers and authors who generously contributed their quotes and stories to this project.

For their patience in listening to me talk about *the book* and for their loving support, I say thank you to my friends Patty Lynn Pancho, Larry Benson, Kerry Coughlin, Jan and Ron Schwert, Garnett Hundley and Patty Zeitlin.

To my mom, Julie Klemanowicz, I offer my loving appreciation and respect for the many ways she has loved and supported me and for the values she has always embodied—*perseverance, honesty, resourcefulness, intelligence* and *courage*.

A special thanks to Dr. Marshall B. Rosenberg for his permission to reprint his *Three Components of Appreciation* from his *book Nonviolent Communication, A Language of Compassion.* I had the good fortune to meet and study with Dr. Rosenberg just as I was completing *The Loving*

Dictionary. The timing was fortuitous. His *Three Components* was a missing element and a valuable contribution to the book.

My sincere thanks to Jack Canfield, co-author of the well-known *Chicken Soup for the Soul* series, for writing the Preface to *The Loving Dictionary*. I was introduced to Jack just as I began working on this book six years ago. His belief in the project and the Preface that he wrote became a shining beacon that lit the long road to completion.

To my real-life guardian angel and long-time mentor, Garth Alley, I give my prayerful thanks. His spiritual and emotional guidance picked me up each time I stumbled. When I got discouraged, his words gave me hope. When I got scared, his words renewed my confidence. When I got tired, his words refreshed my spirit. He was modeling the principals in *The Loving Dictionary* even as I wrote it.

Ultimately, I'm grateful to God for entrusting me with this project and for creating all the coincidences that brought me just the right people I needed at just the right time.

INTRODUCTION

There are 3 billion people that go to bed hungry for food every night, but there are 4 billion people that go to bed hungry for praise or appreciation every night. Cavett Robert

My idea for *The Loving Dictionary* was conceived over dinner with a group of friends, including my good friend Moe Vesey. An animated, vivacious woman, Moe was very excited about a simple word game she and her boyfriend had serendipitously discovered while hiking. Her boyfriend would pick a letter from the alphabet, and she would come up with as many positive words to describe him as she could think of that started with that letter. If he chose the letter *C*, for example, she'd respond with words like *caring, charitable, charming.* Then she would pick a letter and he would do the same for her.

In the process they identified a lot of good things about each other—things they had always taken notice of but had never expressed verbally. Moe described how great it had felt to hear so many good things about herself, especially from someone she cared about. She talked about how valued she felt, about how much closer and trusting they had become.

The rest of us listened attentively, but it became clear to Moe that we weren't fully *getting it*. So over dessert she had each of us pick a letter. As the words poured from one to the other—*dedicated, loyal, wise, persevering, lovable*—a buzz of energy and excitement grew in each one of us. Posture lifted, eyes sparkled and smiles beamed.

I realized that what we were witnessing was the incredible power of words at work. We were experiencing the esteeming impact of appreciation. Moe had made her point. We were all good friends, but we had never expressed even half the wonderful things that we knew and valued about each other. In my WORDpower™ training programs for proactive communication skills, I frequently use the expression *You can't know what you don't know until you know it!* Though each man and woman at the table that night was fairly successful, none of us had known just how hungry we were for appreciation until we got a taste of it.

I had chosen the letter *I*. My friends had responded enthusiastically with *imaginative, interesting, intelligent*. Then someone used a word I had never heard before—*indefatigable.* When someone explained to me what it meant, I almost cried. Despite many accomplishments, I had been struggling with fear and self-doubt my whole life and had always worked extra hard to prove my worth.

I flashed back to myself as a young adult asking my mom why she had never told me how *pretty, smart* or *capable* I was. With innocence she had replied, "I didn't want to give you a big head," then added, "but I told everyone we knew how proud I was of you." How many times have I heard the same story from others! And over and over again the same refrain: "But you never told *me*." Surely no one had ever told our parents either.

Before I left the table that night I was committed to creating *The Loving Dictionary*. That simple word game, which I now call *Gimme An A,* had made me keenly aware of three things: how powerful our words are, how hungry we are for appreciation...and how limited our vocabularies are for expressing that appreciation. That night at dinner we had run out of words!

My intention for *The Loving Dictionary* was to offer as many positive adjectives as I could find for expressing appreciation. The "Dictionary of Appreciation", which contains 1,001 positive adjectives, is followed by two sections: my best insights and reflections on "The Art of Appreciation" are in Part II, and a collection of "Creative Ways to Express Appreciation" is in Part III.

As excited as I was, I had no idea what I was getting myself into when I decided to produce *The Loving Dictionary.* It seemed simple enough—a short book about appreciation and an alphabet of positive adjectives. I soon learned that even the simplest idea can be extremely complicated to execute. So many times I felt overwhelmed with all the details, the countless fits and starts. I wondered if I would ever complete this book; then, nearing completion, I wondered if it would really make a difference or if anyone would care what I had to say about appreciation.

Yet each time I introduced *Gimme An A* to participants in my burgeoning WORDpower™ programs, each time I witnessed the life energy these words unleashed in people, I knew I was on the right track. And each time I experienced the power of appreciation myself I kept going.

I offer you now *The Loving Dictionary* with love and joy. I invite you to use it wisely, use it lovingly...and, please, use it often.

PART I

THE DICTIONARY OF APPRECIATION

WELCOME TO THE DICTIONARY OF APPRECIATION

God put something noble and good in every heart His hand created.
Mark Twain

This Dictionary of Appreciation has 1,001 positive adjectives for expressing appreciation. The words describe the qualities and experiences of people. For instance, Patty Lynn is a very *talented* singer. Her voice is *powerful*. It's *exciting* to listen to her. Each adjective has been succinctly defined and appended with a list of synonyms. Where needed I have added a sentence or phrase to clarify usage. When a word has multiple meanings, I have chosen the most relevant meanings for the purposes of this book.

As we redefine the roles of men and women in our changing culture, our language has been slow to respond. I am hoping to quicken the pace. Currently, reference books that list synonyms for words like *courageous, brave* or *valiant*, include the word *manly* in the synonyms but not the word *womanly*. Knowing my own courage and that of many other women, I have chosen to append the word *womanly* to these wonderful adjectives. As I know and experience more and more men of great kindness and compassion, I have chosen to include paternal qualities, such as *caring, protective* and *loving,* in the synonyms for *manly* along with the traditional ones such as *virile*, *strong* and *gallant*. Likewise, along with the usual synonyms for *womanly*, such as *feminine, tender* and *kind*, I have included qualities such as *courageous, enduring* and *indomitable*, to reflect their qualities in leadership and their triumphs in sports. My intention is to be all inclusive for both genders; to expand the way we define ourselves as women and men; and to reflect the multidimensional, multitalented people we were created to be.

I took creative license with "X" because there are no positive adjectives in current usage that begin with that letter. To assure that people, schools or companies with the initial X in their name are not excluded from certain word games, I have listed under X adjectives that begin with "EX." (The *ex* is italicized to mark the distinction.) For example then, someone named Xavier might be described as *ex*uberant, *ex*pert and *ex*troverted.

While there are no positive adjectives in current usage beginning with the letter X, I did discover one that has fallen into disuse: *xenodochial.* It means open and receptive to strangers or foreigners; hospitable, congenial, broad-minded, unbiased. I have chosen to resurrect this wonderful word and include it in *The Loving Dictionary* because it represents the essence of this book.

While the word *xenodochial* has become archaic, its antonym, *xenophobic* has survived and is in common usage. *Xenophobic* means fearful of strangers or foreigners; unsociable, fearful, narrow-minded, racist. Amazingly, the English language has fewer positive adjectives than negative ones.

We need more positive words in our world. I invite you to do your own research and if you discover a positive word of appreciation that has become archaic, bring it back to life. Or take your own creative license and make up new positive adjectives. When you do, define them, give them synonyms and send them to me for the next edition of *The Loving Dictionary*

A

ablaze
keenly excited or interested; aflame, afire, animated, eager, enthusiastic, ardent, fervent, intense, passionate, impassioned, inspired, exhilarated.

able
having the ability, intelligence or skill to perform well; adept, apt, capable, competent, experienced, accomplished, skillful, masterful, facile, polished, finished, proficient, effective, topnotch, gifted, talented, clever, ingenious, inventive, sage, smart, learned, knowledgeable.

able-bodied
physically healthy and strong; able, athletic, burly, hale, hearty, husky, powerful, robust, rugged, solid, stalwart, well-built, strapping, sturdy, vigorous.

aboveboard
without disguise or trickery; candid, straightforward, direct, forthright, open, outspoken, frank, simple, square, fair, honorable, ingenuous, veracious, honest, r respectable, eputable, creditable, estimable, sincere, true, genuine, guileless, decent, upright, upstanding.

absorbing
arresting the full attention or interest of; amusing, interesting, exciting, winning, fascinating, captivating, engrossing, charming, engaging, arresting, pleasing.

abundant
having more than enough; plentiful, bountiful, wealthy, fertile, fecund, prolific, prosperous, rich, affluent.

accepting
being favorably disposed toward; welcoming, confirming, affirming, validating.

accessible
easily approached; approachable, welcoming, available, responsive, congenial, warm, friendly, genial, affable, pleasant, gracious, easy, polite, agreeable.

acclaimed
praised enthusiastically; honored, praised, celebrated, venerated, exalted.

accommodating
eager to help; cooperative, amiable, agreeable, obliging, yielding, benign, adaptable, warm, kind, generous, helpful, charitable, benevolent, humane, thoughtful, considerate, sympathetic, friendly, cordial, pleasant, gracious.

accomplished
proficient as a result of study and practice; skilled, finished, practiced, expert, proficient, professional, apt, masterful, adept, talented, gifted, clever, facile, learned, versed.

accountable
being responsible for; responsible, answerable, dependable, honorable.

active
1. full of action and energy; vital, lively, dynamic, vibrant, energetic, vivacious, chipper, spirited, peppy, animated, sprightly, spry, quick, agile, alert. **2.** given to purposeful activity; industrious, persevering, studious, diligent.

acute
1. having a keen or discerning intellect; penetrating, discerning, astute, clever, smart, sharp, brainy, bright, intelligent, ingenious, wise, sapient, sagacious, discriminating, perceptive, intuitive: *an acute mind.* **2.** very sensitive; keen, sensitive: *acute hearing.*

adaptable
capable of adapting; flexible, amenable, agreeable, obliging, yielding, accommodating.

adept
having a high degree of knowledge or skill; able, capable, competent, expert, masterly, proficient, skillful, topnotch, good, polished, talented, experienced, accomplished, versed.

admirable
deserving of admiration; laudable, commendable, praiseworthy, meritorious, deserving, creditable, reputable, valuable, honorable, estimable, esteemed, revered, noble, respected, honored, excellent, great, superior, masterly, first-class.

adorable
deserving of adoration; lovable, dear, sweet, cute, darling, precious, cherishable, treasured, beloved, charming, engaging, captivating, enchanting, appealing, delightful, lovely, attractive.

adored
regarded with much admiration and love; loved, beloved, cherished, esteemed, valued, revered, admired, treasured.

adroit
possessing skill and ease in performance; clever, inventive, ingenious, dexterous, nimble, neat, skillful, artful, masterly, deft, quick, handy, agile, lively, facile.

adult
having reached maturity; mature, developed, sensible, judicious, prudent, responsible, dependable.

adventurous
willing to take risks; adventuresome, venturesome, audacious, daring, bold, heroic, enterprising, gallant, chivalrous, valorous, dauntless, plucky, courageous, intrepid, spunky, spirited, fearless, brave.

aesthetic
marked by good taste or sensitivity to beauty; cultured, cultivated, polished, refined, discriminating, aware, artistic: *Erma's aesthetic appreciation of their old house was comforting to the sellers.*

affable
easy to speak to and approach; gracious, genial, approachable, congenial, accessible, sociable, friendly, agreeable, cordial, easy, amicable, mannerly, courteous, amiable, pleasant, obliging, good-natured, good-tempered, benign.

affectionate
feeling or expressing affection; loving, caring, giving, solicitous, devoted, warm, tender, sweet, friendly, amiable, kind.

affective
expressing or causing emotion; emotive, emotional, stirring, touching, moving: *the affective portrayal by the actor.*

affirming
expressing validation for; accepting, esteeming, validating, confirming.

affluent
marked by abundance; prosperous, rich, wealthy, abundant, thriving, flourishing.

afire
keenly excited or interested; ablaze, aflame, animated, enthusiastic, eager, fervent, ardent, passionate, impassioned, inspired, exhilarated.

ageless
never growing old; youthful, young, buoyant, optimistic, cheerful.

agile
moving or thinking quickly and easily; active, alive, deft, lively, brisk, facile, nimble, spry, lithe, well-coordinated, quick, supple, alert, keen, quick-witted, sharp, bright, smart, acute.

aglow
glowing with joy, enthusiasm or love; glowing, beaming, radiant, shining, sunny, bright, cheerful, happy, pleased, gay, glad, gleeful, joyful, blissful, bubbly, sparkling, winsome, convivial, light-hearted, animated, enthusiastic, excited, elated, playful, frolicsome, mirthful.

agreeable
willing and amiable in nature; genial, congenial, kind, cordial, amicable, affable, gracious, couthie, mannerly, courteous, gentle, friendly, pleasant, appealing, likable, good-natured, amenable, yielding, accommodating.

airy
light in manner or movement; buoyant, perky, lively, breezy, debonair, animated, vivacious, cheerful, blithe, gay, merry, jolly, jovial, jocund, jaunty, lithe, agile, nimble, lissome, graceful.

alert
moving or thinking quickly and easily; swift, quick, fast, speedy, agile, nimble, brisk, sprightly, lively, spry, alive, vivacious, animated, active, spirited, frisky, intelligent, smart, bright, clever, keen, attentive, sharp-witted, vigilant, watchful, aware, prepared, mindful, prudent, discreet, careful, circumspect.

alive
1. full of life and active; animated, lively, vibrant, dynamic, energetic, vital, vivacious, vigorous, robust, spry, peppy, active, frisky, spirited, sprightly. **2.** marked by cognizance or perception; aware, wise, sensible, perceptive, awake, keen, cognizant, mindful, knowing.

alluring
very appealing to the mind or eye; appealing, charming, captivating, winning, fascinating, enchanting, bewitching, irresistible, magnetic, ravishing, attractive, beautiful.

altruistic
showing unselfish concern for the welfare of others; humanitarian, humane, beneficent, benevolent, public-spirited, philanthropic, charitable, liberal, magnanimous, unselfish, kind, kind-hearted, generous, big-hearted.

amazing
affecting great wonder or surprise; astonishing, surprising, fabulous, fantastic, remarkable, stupendous, marvelous, wonderful, incredible.

ambitious
marked by ambition; enterprising, striving, driving, energetic, fervent, ardent, earnest, zealous, eager, avid, enthusiastic, spirited, bold, daring.

amenable
open to advice or suggestion; open, responsive, receptive, open-minded, agreeable, amiable, flexible, yielding, reasonable, accommodating.

amiable
having a pleasing and kindly nature; likable, nice, pleasant, sweet, kind, good-natured, agreeable, amenable, understanding, obliging, engaging, accommodating, appealing, winning, charming, gentle, genial, courteous, polite, amicable, friendly, congenial, open, sociable, affable, easygoing.

amicable
showing friendliness or goodwill; friendly, congenial, companionable, neighborly, sociable, approachable, open, easygoing, outgoing, affable, amiable, good-natured, pleasant, nice, charming, winning, mannerly, gracious, understanding, agreeable, warm-hearted, accommodating, amenable, obliging, sympathetic, benign, kindly, peaceable.

amusing
marked by laughter, enjoyment or happiness; entertaining, pleasing, funny, humorous, interesting, lively, absorbing, beguiling, engrossing, sportive, comic, droll, laughable, risible, zany, witty, farcical, jocular.

analytical
able to reason validly; analytic, logical, rational, inquisitive, questioning.

angelic
befitting or like an angel; good, kindly, beautiful, adorable, lovely, exquisite, delicate, virtuous, pure, chaste, holy, pious, spiritual: *an angelic disposition.*

animated
full of life, action or spirit; alive, vital, lively, bright, alert, vivacious, bouncy, sprightly, chipper, spirited, energetic, dynamic, impassioned, ardent, fervent, passionate, radiant, sunny, glowing, bright-eyed, eager, excited, elated, ecstatic, jubilant, enthusiastic, happy, blithe, merry, gay, joyful, ebullient, buoyant, cheerful, jocund, playful, sportive, mirthful, frolicsome.

appealing
attractive to the mind or eye; attractive, charismatic, magnetic, charming, enchanting, inviting, alluring, fascinating, enticing.

appreciative
expressing gratitude or admiration; grateful, thankful, esteeming, affirming, validating.

approachable
easily approached; warm, friendly, accessible, responsive, welcoming, affable, sociable, agreeable, open, communicative, genial, congenial, informal, easygoing.

apt
quick to learn or comprehend; astute, intelligent, clever, ingenious, brilliant, bright, sharp, sagacious, talented, gifted, adroit, quick, facile, proficient, first-rate, able, agile, competent, adept, capable.

ardent
expressing intense feeling; fervent, fervid, passionate, impassioned, fiery, emotional, emotive, excited, enthusiastic, eager, zealous, spirited.

arresting
capturing the attention of; stunning, striking, electrifying, outstanding, dazzling, exciting, extraordinary, remarkable, noteworthy, singular.

articulate
said or presented in clear, effective language; clear, definite, expressive, eloquent, fluent, well-spoken.

artistic
1. showing imagination or skill; skilled, talented, accomplished, proficient, apt, adept, masterly, expert, clever, good, excellent. **2.** marked by good taste; cultivated, cultured, polished, refined, sensitive, elegant, aesthetic, tasteful.

assertive
marked by confident assertion; positive, confident, assured, sure, certain, daring, outspoken.

assiduous
working diligently; persevering, diligent, sedulous, industrious, intent, attentive, studious, earnest, devoted, zealous.

assured
having a firm belief in oneself; confident, secure, self-possessed, self-assured, steady, unwavering.

astonishing
causing sudden wonder or surprise; surprising, amazing, astounding, wonderful, marvelous, awesome.

astounding
causing such surprise as to stun; stunning, surprising, astonishing, amazing, startling, wondrous.

astute
marked by a keen discernment or resourcefulness; sagacious, sapient, wise, shrewd, knowing, perceptive, perspicacious, judicious, thoughtful, discriminating, discreet, prudent, politic, mindful, sensible, sharp, acute, keen, quick, alert, intelligent, smart, bright, clever, ingenious.

athletic
physically strong and active; sinewy, muscular, able-bodied, well-built, vigorous, strapping, robust, hardy, hale, sound, firm, solid, brawny, burly, stalwart.

attentive
giving attention or care to; heedful, observant, watchful, aware, mindful, alert, vigilant, sharp, thoughtful, regardful, gracious, kind, polite, gallant, solicitous, considerate, deferential, accommodating, courteous, respectful.

attractive
appealing to the eye or mind; handsome, beautiful, fair, lovely, pretty, gorgeous, good-looking, pulchritudinous, comely, cute, sweet, elegant, striking, stunning, ravishing, fetching, enchanting, winning, charming, pleasing, engaging, alluring, interesting, captivating, bewitching.

audacious
1. extremely bold or daring; fearless, brave, courageous, adventurous, doughty, intrepid, venturesome, mettlesome, gallant, valiant, heroic, stout, lionhearted, stalwart, plucky, spirited. **2.** extremely original; imaginative, novel, inventive, progressive, unconventional, advanced.

authentic
worthy of trust, reliance or belief; trustworthy, reliable, dependable, credible, genuine, real, truthful, veracious, honest.

autonomous
independent in mind or judgment; free, independent, empowered, self-governing, self-directing.

available
easily approached; approachable, warm, accessible, responsive, open, welcoming, friendly, genial, affable, sociable, courteous, gracious.

avant-garde
daring or new in ideas or styles; innovative, imaginative, creative, modern, progressive, advanced, new, unique, novel, original, unconventional.

avid
having intense desire or interest; keen, enthusiastic, fervent, eager, ardent, excited, energetic, lively, spirited, vivacious, exuberant, wholehearted, earnest, devoted.

awake
marked by awareness or cognizance; aware, vigilant, watchful, observant, attentive, sharp, alert, heedful, alive, wise, sensible, mindful, cognizant.

aware
characterized by cognizance or comprehension; awake, attentive, alert, mindful, heedful, observant, cognizant, knowing, discriminating, percipient, enlightened, informed, knowledgeable, conversant, versed, quick, sharp, intelligent, urbane, sophisticated.

awesome
inspiring awe; outstanding, moving, impressive, tremendous, marvelous, fantastic, remarkable, regal, stately, majestic, sublime, august, noble.

B

balanced
marked by good judgment or equanimity; prudent, judicious, sensible, reasonable, sane, sound, rational, sagacious, sapient, wise, sage, perspicacious, level-headed, commonsensical, calm, collected, cool, composed, self-possessed, poised, steady, consistent, well-balanced, grounded.

beaming
radiant with joy, love or enthusiasm; glowing, aglow, sunny, radiant, bright, cheery, happy, gay, glad, pleased, delighted, blissful, gleeful, joyful, bubbly, sparkling, winsome, light-hearted, convivial, animated, frolicsome, playful, mirthful, enthusiastic, excited, elated.

beautiful
1. especially pleasing to the eye or mind; beauteous, handsome, fair, pretty, comely, becoming, attractive, pulchritudinous, good-looking, ravishing, engaging, enchanting, alluring, enticing, bewitching, charming, elegant, graceful, artistic, delicate. **2.** excellent of it's kind; excellent, gorgeous, exquisite, superb, fine, first-class.

becoming
1. attractive or pleasing to the eye; attractive, handsome, beautiful, comely, stylish, fashionable, chic. **2.** proper and seemly; decent, modest, decorous, mannerly, respectful, refined, polished, polite.

beloved
loved dearly; dear, precious, darling, cherished, loved, valued, respected, adored, treasured, esteemed, prized.

beneficent
promoting or performing acts of kindness or charity; benefic, kindly, charitable, unselfish, benevolent, altruistic, helpful, philanthropic, humane, benignant, benign, good, kind, loving, gracious, considerate, chivalrous, merciful, sympathetic, generous, munificent: *Patty's beneficent support made the conference possible.*

benevolent
characterized by acts of kindness and concern for others; humane, loving, kindly, humanitarian, benign, altruistic, good, caring, beneficent, benignant, charitable, munificent, generous, broad-minded, liberal, unselfish, considerate, understanding, thoughtful, merciful, clement, lenient, compassionate, gentle, tender, helpful, friendly, neighborly.

benign
showing or having a kindly disposition; kind, humane, loving, big, good-hearted, cordial, amiable, amicable, friendly, beneficent, benignant, humanitarian, helpful, altruistic, unselfish, gracious, considerate, thoughtful, gentle, compassionate, tender, lenient, merciful, clement, forbearing, forgiving, understanding.

benignant
marked by kindness toward others; benign, benevolent, gracious, open, generous, charitable, altruistic, unselfish, considerate, thoughtful, compassionate.

bewitching
charming or fascinating; enchanting, captivating, fetching, entrancing, alluring, enticing, appealing, engaging, winning.

big
1. characterized by prominence; notable, prominent, influential, famous, eminent, distinguished, renowned, illustrious, honorable, esteemed, important, powerful, noble, outstanding. **2.** marked by kindness or generosity; gracious, benevolent, beneficent, altruistic, kind-hearted, humane, fair, just, unbiased, forgiving, magnanimous, chivalrous, munificent, generous.

big-hearted
marked by generosity and kindness; generous, magnanimous, kindly, unselfish, big, gracious, benefic, beneficent, benevolent, humane, forgiving, chivalrous, altruistic.

blessed
characterized by happiness or good fortune; fortunate, lucky, content, happy, joyful, cheery, sunny, blithe.

blissful
abounding in bliss; elated, jubilant, ecstatic, delighted, pleased, happy, jolly, gay, cheerful, joyous, gleeful.

blithe
having a light-hearted or carefree disposition; blithesome, cheery, happy, gay, gleeful, joyous, elated, buoyant, merry, jolly, jocund, lively, sprightly, airy, breezy, frisky, jaunty, debonair, enthusiastic, animated, playful, sportive, mirthful, sunny, optimistic, outgoing, convivial.

blooming
full of health, beauty or vigor; thriving, flourishing, blossoming, glowing, radiant, robust, vigorous, sound, healthy.

bold
marked by courage and bravery; brave, heroic, fearless, gallant, daring, courageous, unafraid, dauntless, intrepid, adventurous, valiant, mettlesome, undaunted, assured, confident, audacious, resolute, doughty, game, plucky, valorous, lionhearted, stalwart.

bonny
1. pleasing in appearance; attractive, sweet, pretty, handsome, healthy, lively: *a bonny child.* **2.** pleasing to the senses; pleasant, agreeable, fine: *a bonny day.*

bouncy
alert and high-spirited; lively, energetic, vivacious, chipper, spirited, animated, dashing.

bountiful
1. marked by abundance; abundant, bounteous, prosperous, plentiful, rich. **2.** freely giving; generous, munificent, unsparing, benevolent, magnanimous, beneficent, kind, good, big-hearted, charitable, altruistic, philanthropic.

brainy
marked by intelligence; intelligent, smart, intellectual, knowledgeable, clever, bright, quick, keen, sharp.

brave
characterized by courage and valor; bold, heroic, fearless, chivalrous, gallant, courageous, adventurous, dashing, unafraid, daring, dauntless, intrepid, mettlesome, valorous, game, audacious, plucky, doughty, determined, steadfast, resolved, lionhearted, womanly, manly, stout-hearted, unfaltering, unwavering.

brawny
having strong and well-developed muscles; muscular, sturdy, burly, firm, sinewy, robust, powerful, potent, strong, strapping, solid, stalwart, rugged, hefty, able, wiry, husky, athletic.

breezy
marked by a lively, carefree manner; airy, jaunty, buoyant, debonair, alive, spirited, dynamic, chipper, vivacious, energetic, bright-eyed, sunny, sparkling, peppy, cheery, happy, mirthful, jolly, jovial, gay, glad, light-hearted, enthusiastic, excited, spry, sprightly, active, frisky, frolicsome, playful.

bright
1. mentally quick and original; sharp, intelligent, smart, witty, brainy, clever, alert, keen, astute, acute, quick-witted, resourceful, inventive, ingenious, intellectual, apt, capable, able, gifted, talented, competent, proficient. **2.** showing good spirits; joyous, animated, gay, happy, sunny, cheerful, blithe, light-hearted, alive, lively, spirited, airy, vivacious, buoyant.

brilliant
1. having great intelligence or talent; intelligent, knowledgeable, brainy, bright, intellectual, resourceful, inventive, ingenious, alert, quick, clever, sharp, keen, wise, sapient, sage, perceptive, penetrating, deep, enlightened, scholarly, learned, precocious, talented, accomplished, gifted, proficient, masterful. **2.** done in an outstanding way; splendid, magnificent, glorious, sensational, remarkable, exemplary, dazzling.

broad-minded
tolerant of beliefs, views or behavior that are different from one's own; tolerant, open-minded, liberal, progressive, fair, just, impartial, unbiased, unprejudiced, considerate, magnanimous, benevolent, big, benign, charitable, forbearing, sympathetic, understanding.

brotherly
characteristic of, or befitting brothers; fraternal, affectionate, loyal, kindly, caring, thoughtful, amicable, affable, congenial, genial, sociable, friendly.

bubbly
marked by high spirits; lively, bright, spirited, glowing, bright-eyed, glad, joyful, happy, outgoing, friendly.

buoyant
characterized by a light-hearted nonchalance; happy, merry, jolly, blithe, bright, gay, carefree, lively, vivacious, cheerful, mirthful, gleeful, bubbly, sprightly, peppy, bouncy, airy, jaunty, breezy, debonair.

burly
strong and powerfully built; sturdy, firm, sinewy, robust, strapping, solid, husky, athletic, muscular, brawny, powerful, hardy, rugged, well-built, able-bodied.

businesslike
having characteristics advantageous to business; efficient, effective, systematic, practical, methodical, thorough, orderly, earnest, industrious, diligent, sedulous.

C

calm
not easily excited or flustered; cool, collected, composed, together, easygoing, relaxed, imperturbable, laid-back, casual, even-tempered, unflappable, unruffled, carefree, self-possessed, placid, serene, undisturbed, tranquil, sedate, poised, steady, balanced.

calming
able to calm or quiet; comforting, soothing, consoling, quieting, lulling, gentling.

candid
possessing openness and sincerity of expression; frank, straightforward, forthright, direct, outspoken, free, open, aboveboard, unprejudiced, impartial, unbiased, undisguised, genuine, sincere, ingenuous, guileless, honest.

canny
careful and astute; prudent, discreet, discerning, acute, careful, sensible, keen, alert, observant, astute, aware, shrewd, sharp, wise, sagacious, bright, smart.

capable
possessing the ability to perform well; able, skillful, proficient, adept, efficient, effective, competent, qualified, accomplished, practiced, masterful, apt, dexterous, adroit, intelligent, smart, clever, learned, versed, ingenious, gifted, talented.

captivating
capturing and holding the attention of; charming, fascinating, appealing, alluring, enchanting, engaging, fetching, enticing, bewitching, prepossessing, entrancing.

carefree
without care or worry; light, merry, cheerful, jocund, jolly, gay, joyful, light-hearted, debonair, blithe, jaunty, bouncy, sprightly, lively, spirited, animated.

careful
showing cautious attentiveness; mindful, observant, watchful, heedful, canny, prudent, discreet, judicious, circumspect, vigilant, protective, alert, aware, awake, attentive, solicitous, conscientious, considerate, thoughtful.

caring
marked by concern and empathy for others; loving, attentive, solicitous, thoughtful, kind, kindly, regardful, considerate.

casual
not constrained by rigid standards; easygoing, relaxed, easy, informal, natural, carefree.

catching
possessing the ability to charm; charming, captivating, fascinating, bewitching, fetching, entrancing, enchanting, alluring, winning, intriguing, interesting.

celebrated
widely esteemed and known; notable, distinguished, preeminent, respected, prominent, eminent, great, honored, popular, famed, acclaimed, illustrious, renowned, prestigious, redoubtable.

champion
exceptionally good of its kind; first-rate, first-class, fine, excellent, superior, great, superb, prime, splendid, capital, topnotch.

charismatic
having the power or quality of attracting; appealing, enchanting, alluring, charming, fascinating, attractive, magnetic, glamorous.

charitable
generous in giving help or money to those in need; compassionate, humane, humanitarian, altruistic, benevolent, beneficent, generous, philanthropic, munificent, big-hearted, unselfish, kind, good-natured, considerate, benignant, tolerant, merciful, forbearing, lenient, amiable, understanding, sympathetic, helpful, friendly, obliging, agreeable.

charming
attractive, delightful or fascinating; pretty, beautiful, handsome, lovely, sweet, elegant, graceful, winsome, pleasing, appealing, enchanting, engaging, fetching, captivating, beguiling, bewitching, mesmerizing, alluring, entrancing, prepossessing.

chaste
beyond moral reproach; virtuous, modest, innocent, pure, good, decent, wholesome, honorable, moral, honest, righteous, upright, reputable, creditable.

cheerful
being in or showing good spirits; cheery, happy, bright, sunny, merry, positive, optimistic, glad, blithe, gay, light-hearted, happy-go-lucky, carefree, bubbly, jocund, joyful, amiable, convivial, genial, hearty, lively, chipper, dynamic, mirthful, vivacious, animated, spirited, jaunty, sprightly, frolicsome, playful, aglow, zestful, sparkling, blissful.

cherishable
inviting tender and affectionate care; adorable, lovable, dear, precious, darling, endearing, sweet, lovely, winsome.

cherished
regarded highly; revered, esteemed, loved, adored, valued, appreciated, beloved, respected, treasured, prized.

chic
attractive and fashionable in style; smart, modish, dapper, dashing, stylish, sharp, elegant, classy, natty, well-dressed, spruce, rakish, swank.

childlike
like a child as in innocence or candor; open, innocent, ingenuous, genuine, honest, sincere, natural, trusting, guileless, forthright, straightforward.

chipper
alert and high-spirited; happy, bright, sunny, cheery, merry, light-hearted, positive, optimistic, glad, blithe, carefree, joyous, jocund, happy-go-lucky, genial, convivial, lively, vivacious, spirited, playful, bouncy, dashing, jaunty.

chivalrous
marked by courtesy, courage and honor; chivalric, good, big, kindly, benign, humanitarian, benevolent, gracious, courageous, brave, heroic, intrepid, spirited, valorous, gallant, dauntless, fearless, stately, courtly, knightly, lionhearted, true, steady, principled, faithful, dependable.

circumspect
aware of possible consequences; alert, mindful, careful, heedful, watchful, discreet, cautious, judicious, prudent, discerning, politic, acute, perspicacious, percipient, perceptive.

civilized
characterized by refinement or enlightenment; polite, well-bred, cultivated, cultured, refined, enlightened, polished, urbane.

classic
serving as a standard or model because of it's high quality; superior, masterly, remarkable, excellent, outstanding, first-rate, extraordinary, notable, exemplary, model, ideal, consummate.

classy
of a high class or grade; stylish, elegant, admirable, high-class.

clear
free from uncertainty or doubt; sure, assured, confident, definite, positive, secure, certain, unwavering.

clear-headed
possessing a clear, orderly mind; quick, sharp, astute, smart, bright, shrewd, alert, attentive, observant, collected, steady, calm, composed, self-possessed, sound, thoughtful, sensible, rational, sagacious, wise, judicious, prudent, circumspect, level-headed, discerning.

clement
of a lenient or merciful nature; humane, compassionate, charitable, magnanimous, beneficent, benign, soft, tender, gentle, forgiving, tolerant, forbearing, patient, considerate, sympathetic, kindly, soft-hearted, temperate, liberal.

clever
mentally bright, original and quick; intelligent, smart, brilliant, talented, sharp, apt, resourceful, precocious, ingenious, creative, inventive, acute, keen, shrewd, ready, sharp-witted, quick, facile, agile, masterful, capable, efficient, adept, witty, whimsical, sparkling, scintillating.

cognizant
characterized by perception and comprehension; aware, awake, quick, sharp, observant, mindful, perceptive, percipient, discerning, knowing, sensible, wise, intelligent, versed, enlightened, conversant, informed, knowledgeable, urbane, sophisticated.

collaborative
working together toward a common end; cooperative, synergetic.

collected
serenely self-assured; cool-headed, calm, imperturbable, serene, placid, cool, even-tempered, self-possessed, unruffled, together.

colorful
vividly distinctive; bright, gay, vivid, striking, vibrant, animated, dynamic, impressive, eccentric.

comedic
having a comic nature; comical, funny, amusing, humorous, witty, entertaining, droll, laughable, zany.

comely
1. wholesome and pleasing to the eye; beautiful, handsome, lovely, pretty, bonny, attractive, good-looking, fair, winsome, appealing, glowing, radiant. **2.** proper and seemly; decent, becoming, modest, decorous, mannerly, respectful, refined, polite, respectable: *comely behavior.*

comforting
able to promote emotional or physical ease; soothing, calming, consoling, gladdening, reassuring, encouraging.

comical
arousing mirth or amusement; funny, witty, humorous, amusing, comedic, comic, entertaining, droll, laughable, risible, zany.

commanding
possessing the power to command attention or respect; impressive, noble, majestic, august, imposing, compelling, powerful, self-assured, self-confident.

commendable
deserving of praise; praiseworthy, worthy, good, admirable, estimable, meritorious, laudable, deserving, reputable, respectable, honorable, virtuous, righteous, just, principled, upright, excellent, exemplary, noble.

committed
pledged to a particular thought or action; devoted, dedicated, loyal, determined, faithful, true, earnest.

commonsensical
exhibiting sound, practical judgment; reasonable, sensible, rational, solid, astute, logical, sane, prudent, judicious, just, intelligent, wise, sage, sagacious, balanced, level-headed, well-founded, well-grounded: *a commonsensical solution.*

communicative
ready to talk and share information; free, open, candid, straightforward, frank, conversable, approachable, accessible.

companionable
possessing the qualities of a good companion; congenial, friendly, affable, cooperative, convivial, social, amiable, warm, hearty, jolly, gregarious, sociable, hospitable, genial, charming, cordial, polite, courteous, agreeable, pleasant.

compassionate
expressing concern for human welfare and suffering; humane, charitable, benevolent, benign, beneficent, kind, humanitarian, liberal, understanding, tolerant, considerate, tender, good, loving, gentle, mild, easy, patient, gracious, lenient, merciful, clement, forgiving, magnanimous, chivalrous.

compatible
existing together harmoniously; agreeable, amiable, congenial, genial, friendly, cordial, amicable, cooperative, harmonious.

compelling
having a powerful effect or influence; stirring, inspiring, arousing, stimulating, thrilling, moving, motivating, captivating, touching, poignant.

competent
having enough ability or knowledge; able, capable, masterful, expert, polished, accomplished, practiced, experienced, effective, skillful, good, proficient, adept, qualified, knowledgeable, versed, conversant, savvy, well-informed.

complete
having all the required skills or characteristics; accomplished, skilled, polished, fulfilled, whole, consummate, perfect, exemplary: *a complete scholar.*

complimentary
expressing compliments; laudatory, acclamatory, ingratiating, flattering.

composed
serenely self-assured; collected, cool, calm, imperturbable, cool-headed, self-possessed, together, sedate, poised, balanced, easygoing, even-tempered, serene, tranquil, steady, unruffled.

confident
characterized by strong belief or assurance; secure, assured, sure, certain, positive, self-assured, self-confident, self-possessed, steady, steadfast, unwavering, unflinching.

congenial
having a kind and agreeable nature; gracious, cordial, nice, affable, genial, sociable, sweet, friendly, harmonious, companionable, kind, amicable, couthie, good-natured, cooperative, easygoing, pleasant, neighborly, hospitable.

congruent
agreeing in all ways; congruous, harmonious, consistent: *She is congruent in word and deed.*

conscientious
1. guided by conscience to do what is right; conscionable, principled, moral, ethical, upright, righteous, upstanding, sincere, good, honest, just, true, earnest, dedicated, loyal, devoted, faithful. **2.** marked by thoroughness; thorough, precise, particular, scrupulous, accurate, meticulous, detailed, methodical.

consequential
possessing considerable influence; important, powerful, influential, impressive, noteworthy, notable: *a consequential member of the senate.*

considerate
having concern for the well-being of others; thoughtful, polite, courteous, solicitous, attentive, aware, mindful, gallant, patient, compassionate, kind, sympathetic, tender-hearted, benign, beneficent, benevolent, charitable, generous, unselfish, friendly, neighborly.

consistent
constantly adhering to the same principles; dependable, reliable, steady, congruous, congruent, harmonious, devoted, faithful, persistent, loyal.

consoling
promoting comfort or cheer; soothing, comforting, calming, reassuring, gladdening, encouraging.

constant
unswerving in devotion, love or duty; true, firm, steady, fast, solid, stable, loyal, faithful, devoted, trustworthy, reliable, dependable, determined, resolute, unfaltering, unwavering, staunch, indomitable, persevering, persistent, industrious, indefatigable, assiduous, sedulous, plucky, steadfast.

content
satisfied with what one has or is; happy, glad, cheerful, sunny, calm, peaceful, carefree, relaxed, serene, easygoing, placid.

conversable
easy to talk with; approachable, receptive, agreeable, amenable, open, obliging, accommodating, free, unreserved, frank, candid, straightforward, communicative.

conversant
familiar with by study or use; learned, well-informed, versed, skilled, practiced, proficient, knowledgeable.

conversational
liking or given to conversation; communicative, conversable, unreserved, free, open, candid, straightforward, frank.

convincing
possessing the power to convince; persuasive, impressive, effective, compelling, impelling.

convivial
enjoying good company; sociable, social, companionable, friendly, cordial, genial, congenial, hearty, gregarious, hospitable, jovial, cheerful, joyful.

cool
not easily excited or flustered; calm, collected, composed, imperturbable, easygoing, together, relaxed, sedate, unruffled, unflappable, level-headed, self-possessed, even-tempered.

cool-headed
not easily disturbed; collected, cool, calm, unflappable, self-controlled, imperturbable, unruffled.

cooperative
willing to cooperate; collaborative, helpful, obliging, accommodating.

cordial
having a kind and friendly nature; gracious, congenial, genial, affable, sociable, warm, pleasant, couthie, affectionate, easy, agreeable, good-natured, amiable, easygoing, sincere.

cosmopolitan
broad-minded in attitude, viewpoint or interest; broad-minded, worldly, cultivated, urbane, metropolitan, liberal, cultured, sophisticated, worldly-wise.

courageous
characterized by courage and valor; bold, heroic, fearless, gallant, brave, chivalrous, dashing, adventurous, unafraid, daring, dauntless, stout, gutsy, intrepid, mettlesome, valiant, audacious, doughty, determined, steadfast, resolved, plucky, game, manly, womanly, stout-hearted, lionhearted, unfaltering.

courteous
marked by good manners; polite, genteel, well-bred, well-mannered, thoughtful, deferential, respectful, decorous, attentive, tactful, politic, diplomatic, cordial, genial, affable, pleasant, agreeable, gallant, courtly, chivalric, considerate, obliging, ingratiating, gracious, ladylike, gentlemanly, urbane, debonair.

courtly
marked by elaborate and formal courtesy; gracious, gallant, stately, chivalrous, knightly, chivalric, well-bred, refined, polished, elegant, urbane, sophisticated, debonair, suave, polite, mannerly, respectful, proper, decorous, deferential.

couthie
having an agreeable nature genial, amiable, amenable, friendly, kindly: *The couthie innkeeper made his guests feel at home.*

creative
characterized by originality and expressiveness; original, ingenious, imaginative, resourceful, inventive, innovative, artistic, clever, inspired, adept, accomplished, talented, gifted, skilled.

credible
worthy of belief or confidence; honest, truthful, ethical, veracious, creditable, scrupulous, believable, forthright, straightforward, trustworthy, dependable.

creditable
deserving of honor or credit; worthy, praiseworthy, estimable, admirable, commendable, laudable, meritorious, honorable, respectable, reputable, trustworthy, dependable, reliable: *Jan made a creditable effort to implement all of the last minute changes.*

cuddly
inviting an affectionate embrace; huggable, embraceable.

cultivated
marked by discriminating taste and knowledge; cultured, civilized, well-bred, enlightened, polished, refined, urbane, educated, finished, trained.

cultured
showing or having culture; refined, educated, polished, thoroughbred, well-bred, cultivated, sophisticated, genteel, urbane, cosmopolitan, gracious, elegant.

curious
eager to learn or know; inquisitive, inquiring, questioning, searching.

cute
pleasingly pretty or attractive; fetching, appealing, charming, sweet, adorable, dear, darling, precious

D

daedel
physically or mentally adept; deft, adroit, nimble, agile, quick, facile, proficient, skillful, experienced, masterful, clever, resourceful, ingenious, inventive.

dainty
marked by delicate beauty or grace; beautiful, pretty, lovely, attractive, fair, comely, charming, fetching, fine, delicate, elegant, graceful.

dandy
something very good; excellent, fine, good, great, exceptional, superior, splendid, superb, first-class, capital, champion, topflight.

dapper
trim and neat in appearance; smart, natty, spruce, rakish, gay, jaunty, well-dressed, swank, ritzy, snazzy.

daring
willing to take risks; adventurous, bold, adventuresome, venturesome, venturous, brave, valiant, valorous, courageous, fearless, audacious, intrepid, dauntless, undaunted, assertive, spunky, plucky.

darling
regarded dearly with tenderness and love; beloved, cherished, treasured, loved, lovable, adorable, precious, dear, cute, sweet, enchanting, charming, winsome.

dashing
1. high-spirited and brave; brisk, alert, lively, vivacious, bouncy, dynamic, airy, energetic, exuberant, chipper, spirited, animated, gallant, valiant, valorous, adventurous, daring, courageous, mettlesome, fearless, stalwart, venturesome. **2.** very fashionable; chic, smart, stylish, modish, swank, dapper, elegant, sharp, classy, natty, jaunty, spruce.

dauntless
not intimidated or discouraged; bold, brave, heroic, fearless, gallant, valiant, courageous, mettlesome, daring, intrepid, undaunted, game, audacious, doughty, venturesome, stout-hearted, indomitable, resolute, lionhearted, hardy, stalwart, high-spirited, confident.

dazzling
exciting admiration with brilliance or splendor; stunning, astounding, amazing, striking, breathtaking, brilliant, remarkable, fantastic, splendrous, stupendous, marvelous, incredible, sensational, exquisite, magnificent, impressive, gorgeous, resplendent, splendiferous, beautiful: *the dazzling sunset; the dazzling play by the quarterback.*

dear
regarded with love and affection; loved, beloved, cherished, treasured, valued, darling, precious, lovable, adorable.

debonair
gaily courteous and charming; airy, buoyant, jaunty, breezy, light, gay, carefree, light-hearted, blithe, merry, cheery, sunny, vivacious, sprightly, jocund, polite, gracious, urbane, suave, genteel, gallant, chivalrous.

decent
adhering to recognized standards of propriety, modesty or good taste; right, proper, nice, respectable, decorous, becoming, seemly, pure, modest, virtuous, chaste, honest, upright, honorable, trustworthy.

decisive
not hesitating or wavering; sure, definite, positive, certain, resolute, firm, determined, unambiguous, unwavering.

decorous
marked by propriety in behavior, character or appearance; proper, right, nice, comely, respectable, decent, becoming, seemly, polished, refined, genteel, elegant, mannerly, polite, well-behaved, modest, calm, sedate, composed.

dedicated
wholly devoted to a particular task, ideal or goal; committed, faithful, determined, loyal, persevering, true, zealous, earnest, indefatigable.

deep
marked by penetrating intellectual powers; wise, sagacious, sage, learned, scholarly, enlightened, discerning, knowing, perspicacious.

deferential
showing courteous submission or respect; deferent, dutiful, obeisant, yielding, thoughtful, respectful, polite, courteous, regardful.

definite
without any doubt; positive, certain, sure, decisive, explicit, precise, unambiguous, unwavering.

deft
marked by dexterity; adroit, handy, dexterous, nimble, nimble-fingered, agile, light, quick, active, brisk, lively, skilled, skillful, adept, facile, daedel, proficient, experienced.

deliberate
marked by careful consideration; purposeful, determined, resolute, orderly, methodical, systematic, thorough, steady, balanced, prudent, discreet, circumspect.

delicate
1. having tact and skill in dealing with others; discreet, discerning, discriminating, perceptive, tactful, politic, diplomatic, considerate, sensitive. **2.** fine or dainty in quality or form; fine, dainty, exquisite, elegant, choice.

delicious
very delightful or pleasing; pleasing, satisfying, pleasurable, enjoyable, gratifying: *a delicious massage.*

delightful
highly pleasing; delightsome, agreeable, pleasurable, lovely, pleasant, attractive, congenial, amiable, winsome, engaging, inviting, enchanting, charming.

democratic
practicing social equality; fair, impartial.

demonstrative
marked by the open expression of emotion; expressive, emotive, open, communicative, emotional, feeling, loving, warm, affectionate, tender.

demure
modest or reserved in manner; quiet, decorous, seemly, proper, delicate, unpretentious, unassuming.

dependable
able to be depended on; responsible, solid, steady, reliable, trustworthy, honest, honorable, sure, reputable.

deserving
worthy of merit; praiseworthy, laudable, admirable, commendable, creditable, meritorious, exemplary.

desirable
worth desiring; attractive, agreeable, pleasing, captivating, enchanting, engaging, winsome, admirable, estimable, worthy, superb, first-rate, first-class, popular, fine, superior: *Larry's loyalty is a desirable trait to have in a friend.*

determined
not hesitating or wavering; intent, resolute, firm, staunch, steadfast, constant, persevering, devoted, earnest, persistent, purposeful, indomitable.

developed
having reached full maturity or growth; experienced, seasoned, refined, polished, mature, adult: *a keenly developed intuition.*

devoted
1. given to a single purpose; dedicated, persevering, persistent, indefatigable, determined, true, faithful, loyal, earnest, eager, zealous. **2.** displaying strong affection; loving, affectionate, warm, ardent, attentive, tender.

devout
showing reverence or sincerity; holy, pious, reverent, faithful, prayerful, righteous, sincere, earnest, heartfelt, fervent, ardent.

dexterous
physically or mentally adept; adroit, deft, daedel, nimble-fingered, handy, neat, apt, agile, facile, proficient, skillful, masterly, expert, polished, accomplished, ingenious, artistic, inventive, resourceful, clever, keen, sharp, witty.

different
not ordinary; unusual, novel, unique, unconventional, diverse, distinctive, singular, individual, extraordinary, remarkable, notable, exceptional.

dignified
showing or possessing dignity; noble, distinguished, well-bred, genteel, regal, impressive, stately, august, grand.

diligent
marked by persevering attention and effort; industrious, studious, steady, sedulous, assiduous, zealous, intent, earnest, thorough, persevering, tireless, unfaltering, indefatigable.

diplomatic
having tact and skill in dealing with others; sensitive, delicate, politic, discreet, judicious, tactful, prudent, discerning, perspicacious.

direct
speaking freely and sincerely; open, straight, honest, straightforward, frank, forthright, plain-spoken, candid, explicit, unambiguous, clear, outspoken, truthful, ingenuous, aboveboard, uninhibited.

disarming
able to win the favor or confidence of; charming, winning.

discerning
characterized by sound judgment and understanding; wise, sage, sapient, sagacious, discriminating, knowing, selective, astute, acute, perceptive, keen, sharp, alert, quick, perspicacious, judicious, sensitive, discreet, politic, prudent, mindful, thoughtful, sensible, clear-headed, reasonable, intelligent, smart, quick-witted, bright, clever.

disciplined
marked by behavior maintained by training and control; self-directed, self-controlled, trained, practiced.

discreet
having or exhibiting tact and good judgment; tactful, discriminating, prudent, discerning, diplomatic, circumspect, politic, judicious, wise, mindful, sensible, reasonable, sage, sagacious, sapient, astute, aware.

discriminating
1. possessing careful judgment; discreet, discerning, perspicacious, percipient, perceptive, keen. **2.** having fine taste; tasteful, selective, aesthetic, artistic, refined, cultured, cultivated, polished.

distinctive
characterized by individuality; singular, novel, individual, different, unusual, remarkable, noteworthy, unique, unconventional.

distinguished
characterized by excellence; great, famous, prominent, notable, famed, eminent, illustrious, well-known, esteemed, memorable, renowned, preeminent, celebrated, honorable, respected, noble, dignified, genteel, gentle, well-bred.

diverse
having distinct and varied skills and characteristics; versatile, diversified, multifaceted, multidimensional, multitalented, multifarious.

divine
supremely good or beautiful; super, magnificent, heavenly, perfect, lovely, charming, stunning, striking.

doughty
steadfastly courageous; bold, heroic, fearless, adventurous, daring, stout, gutsy, undaunted, valiant, brave, audacious, game, dashing, gallant, chivalrous, lionhearted, mettlesome, intrepid, steadfast, determined, unwavering: *a doughty soldier.*

down-to-earth
being aware of things as they really are; realistic, sensible, objective, practical, judicious, prudent, astute.

dreamy
1. able to soothe or relax; soothing, calming, refreshing. **2.** inspiring delight; wonderful, heavenly, fabulous, terrific.

droll
whimsically amusing; humorous, funny, amusing, comic, comical, laughable, risible, zany, merry, jocular, jocose, witty, entertaining.

dulcet
characterized by soothing harmony of sound; soothing, smooth, sweet, sweet-sounding, flowing, pleasant, golden, harmonious, mellifluous, lyrical, melodic, melodious: *the dulcet tones of his voice.*

dutiful
marked by courteous obedience or respect; respectful, courteous, polite, thoughtful, considerate, righteous, moral, ethical, virtuous, responsible, reliable, faithful, obliging, willing, deferential, accommodating, agreeable.

dynamic
characterized by energy or action; alive, active, vigorous, lively, energetic, brisk, peppy, spry, sprightly, spirited, enterprising, eager, zealous, electric, strong, high-powered, powerful, effective.

E

eager
characterized by intense desire or interest; enthusiastic, spirited, zestful, ardent, solicitous, keen, avid, hopeful, inspired, sanguine, excited, animated, impassioned, sincere, earnest, persevering, studious, diligent, industrious, sedulous, ambitious, enterprising.

eagle-eyed
showing keen observation or attention; keen-sighted, acute, alert, awake, sharp, bright, watchful, vigilant, farseeing, perspicacious, perceptive, intuitive, insightful, discriminating, discerning, wise, prudent, discreet.

earnest
characterized by depth or sincerity of feeling or purpose; fervent, resolute, sincere, serious, zealous, ardent, passionate, impassioned, intent, assiduous, diligent, firm, devoted, purposeful, dedicated, committed, wholehearted.

earthy
unaffected or hearty; natural, direct, robust, uninhibited, unpretentious, open, unassuming, down-to-earth.

easygoing
calm and friendly; agreeable, cordial, genial, congenial, amiable, affable, understanding, tolerant, accepting, good-natured, good-tempered, patient, serene, composed, placid, casual, relaxed, imperturbable.

ebullient
abounding with joy and enthusiasm; exuberant, high-spirited, vivacious, sparkling, effervescent, buoyant, breezy, aglow, enthusiastic, joyful, zestful, exhilarated, irrepressible.

eccentric
deviating from the conventional; unique, unusual, curious, quaint, original, individual, singular, rare, unconventional.

economical
prudent in the management of resources; thrifty, canny, frugal, careful, provident, temperate, moderate, conservative.

ecstatic
characterized by ecstasy; blissful, enraptured, rhapsodic, excited, thrilled, joyful, enthusiastic, radiant, beaming, happy, enchanted.

educated
characterized by culture and knowledge; literate, knowledgeable, enlightened, informed, lettered, learned, scholarly, well-versed, erudite, conversant, intellectual, brainy, accomplished, refined, cultivated, cultured, artistic, broad-minded, articulate, well-spoken.

educational
providing knowledge or skill: enlightening, informative.

effective
producing or capable of producing a desired effect; effectual, efficacious, efficient, capable, competent, able, adept, masterful, skillful, productive, proficient, impressive, powerful, persuasive, stimulating, compelling: *an effective team effort, an effective presentation.*

efficient
performing effectively with skill or economy; skillful, expert, masterful, masterly, accomplished, polished, experienced, clever, adept, effective, productive, proficient, dynamic, energetic, competent, capable, efficacious, effectual, systematic, well-prepared, businesslike.

elated
expressing great joy or pride; excited, exhilarated, thrilled, overjoyed, uplifted, jubilant, triumphant, euphoric, pleased, happy, joyful, gleeful, blissful.

electric
charged with excitement; electrifying, exciting, thrilling, stimulating, stirring, moving, astonishing, astounding.

elegant
1. characterized by good taste and richness; fine, delicate, tasteful, exquisite, grand, graceful, gorgeous, luxurious. **2.** having dignity, grace and refinement; refined, cultivated, cultured, genteel, courteous, urbane, gracious, sophisticated, debonair, suave, dapper, stylish, aesthetic, discriminating, artistic.

elevated
1. of a high intellectual or moral level; noble, admirable, estimable, high-minded, honorable, righteous, moral, principled, meritorious: *elevated thoughts.* **2.** marked by high spirits; exhilarated, inspired, high-spirited, animated, joyful, glad, elated, cheerful, gleeful, blithe.

elfish
like an elf; impish, mischievous, prankish, puckish, pixyish.

eloquent
movingly expressive; articulate, expressive, fluent, well-spoken, impassioned, spirited, persuasive, effective, impelling.

emancipated
free from influence or control; free, liberated, uninhibited, self-governed, independent.

eminent
outstanding in reputation or character; distinguished, prominent, great, famous, renowned, notable, noted, illustrious, preeminent, celebrated, esteemed, important, outstanding, honorable, revered, respected, noble, redoubtable.

emotional
expressing or causing emotion; emotive, expressive, affective, impassioned, ardent, passionate, affectionate, feeling, sentimental, sympathetic, compassionate, warm, loving, moving, stirring, touching.

empathetic
aware of and sensitive to the needs of others; empathic, sympathetic, understanding, feeling, responsive.

empowered
having power or authority over one's own judgments or actions; independent, free, autonomous, self-governed, self-directed, self-reliant.

enchanting
especially appealing to the eye or mind; lovely, pretty, attractive, delightful, sweet, irresistible, magnetic, winsome, fetching, alluring, charming, fascinating, captivating, engaging, entrancing, enticing, bewitching, intriguing.

encouraging
inspiring with confidence; cheering, heartening, buoying, validating, affirming, inspiring, motivating, emboldening.

endearing
inspiring love and affection; lovable, adorable, darling, delightful, sweet, precious, charming, captivating, winning.

energetic
exhibiting, possessing or using energy; active, vigorous, lively, electric, alive, snappy, spirited, animated, dynamic, hardy, robust, chipper, spry, peppy, sprightly, enterprising, diligent, devoted, eager, industrious, ambitious, determined, effective, effectual.

energizing
able to stimulate to physical or emotional activity; invigorating, refreshing, stimulating, enlivening, vitalizing, motivating, uplifting, cheering, inspiring.

engaging
pleasantly appealing to the eye or mind; attractive, handsome, sweet, lovely, pretty, beautiful, graceful, delightful, agreeable, likable, magnetic, irresistible, fetching, alluring, bewitching, beguiling, entrancing, fascinating, captivating, enchanting, mesmerizing.

engrossing
being able to capture and hold the attention of; captivating, fascinating, interesting, mesmerizing, engaging, amusing, charming, enthralling, absorbing.

enjoyable
affording enjoyment; pleasurable, nice, lovely, great, fine, pleasant, delightful, agreeable, satisfying, gratifying, amusing, entertaining.

enlightened
marked by intellectual or spiritual insight; insightful, open-minded, aware, understanding, sensitive, wise, learned, intellectual, scholarly, knowledgeable, literate, informed, versed, conversant, cultivated, well-bred, cultured, urbane.

enlightening
providing knowledge or wisdom; illuminating, informative.

enlivening
serving to make lively or cheerful; vitalizing, stimulating, invigorating, energizing, refreshing, stirring, exciting, thrilling, inspiring, cheering, uplifting.

enrapturing
able to excite or delight greatly; thrilling, fascinating, enchanting, exciting, captivating, bewitching, entrancing.

enterprising
having initiative, imagination and energy; resourceful, productive, self-reliant, imaginative, inventive, creative, ambitious, determined, resolute, earnest, alert, sharp, keen, smart, enthusiastic, eager, ardent, fervent, avid, energetic, spirited, venturesome, adventurous, bold, courageous, daring, brave.

entertaining
agreeably diverting; interesting, engrossing, engaging, amusing, pleasing, funny, laughable, comical, humorous, jocular.

enthralling
capturing and holding the attention of; captivating, charming, arresting, enchanting, bewitching, entrancing, engrossing, absorbing, fascinating, mesmerizing, spellbinding.

enthusiastic
characterized by lively, eager interest; warm, ardent, fervent, keen, impassioned, passionate, zealous, wholehearted, devoted, earnest, excited, animated, glowing, vivacious, exuberant, emotive, spirited, ebullient, expressive.

entrancing
especially appealing to the eye or mind; sweet, lovely, attractive, alluring, charming, enchanting, appealing, fascinating, bewitching, enrapturing, engaging, captivating, prepossessing.

equitable
fair or just; unbiased, impartial, nonjudgmental, reasonable, fair-minded, even-handed, broad-minded, neutral, judicious.

erudite
characterized by knowledge and scholarship; knowledgeable, well-read, scholarly, learned, literary, lettered, educated, academic, well-versed, intellectual, knowing, sage, wise, enlightened, cognizant: *an erudite speaker.*

especial
distinct among others of its kind; special, distinctive, singular, unique, unusual, exceptional, outstanding.

esteemed
highly respected; revered, loved, adored, cherished, appreciated, valued, admired, prized, treasured.

esteeming
marked by high regard and respect; affirming, validating, confirming.

esthetic
marked by good taste or sensitivity to beauty; cultured, cultivated, polished, refined, discriminating, aware, artistic.

estimable
deserving of admiration, honor or respect; worthy, commendable, admirable, laudable, meritorious, praiseworthy, respectable, reputable, honorable: *The principal had an estimable reputation for honesty.*

ethical
in accordance with the rules of right or good conduct; moral, proper, right, righteous, principled, right-minded, honest, virtuous, just, fair, upright, decent, straightforward.

euphoric
possessing a feeling of great happiness or well-being; ecstatic, blissful, elated, joyous, jubilant, enraptured, exhilarated.

even-tempered
not easily excited or flustered; cool, collected, composed, together, laid-back, relaxed, calm, imperturbable, easygoing, cool-headed.

excellent
exceptionally good; great, fine, superior, prime, choice, splendid, superb, capital, exceptional, first-class, champion, outstanding, first-rate, superlative, remarkable.

exceptional
far above average; outstanding, magnificent, preeminent, unique, rare, remarkable, extraordinary, phenomenal, singular, superior, excellent.

exciting
able to produce excitement; stirring, moving, inspiring, stimulating, thrilling, motivating, electrifying, captivating, exhilarating.

exemplary
deserving of imitation; admirable, commendable, meritorious, notable, laudable, praiseworthy, noteworthy, model, perfect, ideal, consummate, outstanding, superior, excellent.

exhilarating
enlivening or making cheerful; invigorating, stimulating, exciting, revitalizing, energizing, vitalizing, thrilling, stirring, inspiring, uplifting.

exotic
strikingly unusual or different; unique, novel, singular, striking, impressive, extraordinary, fantastic, remarkable, glamorous, colorful.

experienced
skilled or learned through practice; practiced, accomplished, proficient, skillful, adept, prepared, ready, versed, knowledgeable, competent, capable, able, efficient, professional, good, expert, master, masterly, savvy, sophisticated, worldly, wise.

expert
characterized by a high degree of skill or knowledge; proficient, adept, masterful, skillful, master, professional, polished, practiced, accomplished, experienced, adroit, deft, facile, knowledgeable, learned, well-versed, well-informed.

expressive
conveying meaning or feeling; eloquent, emotive, emotional, passionate, intense.

exquisite
1. having a particular beauty, charm or refinement; beautiful, attractive, striking, handsome, elegant, refined, graceful, delicate. **2.** characterized by great excellence; fine, excellent, rare, precious, choice, superior, select, splendid, outstanding, matchless, incomparable.

extraordinary
beyond what is usual, ordinary or customary; unusual, remarkable, rare, exceptional, singular, unique, special, invaluable, surprising, striking, amazing, phenomenal, astonishing, wondrous, fantastic, fabulous, majestic, prodigious, august, important, eminent, notable.

extroverted
having an outgoing personality; sociable, gregarious, friendly, congenial, amiable.

exuberant
marked by good health and high spirits; high-spirited, vivacious, ebullient, sparkling, effervescent, zesty, buoyant, lively, animated, enthusiastic, energetic.

eye-catching
visually appealing; outstanding, striking, arresting, stunning, dazzling.

F

fabulous
exceptionally unusual or good; amazing, incredible, wonderful, marvelous, fantastic, astonishing, superb, remarkable, unbelievable, stupendous, phenomenal.

facile
exhibiting or possessing skill and ease in performance; proficient, adept, expert, clever, artful, apt, masterful, skilled, handy, deft, adroit, dexterous, nimble.

fair
1. adhering to the accepted rules or standards; sporting, sportsmanlike, square, just. **2.** free from bias in judgment; objective, equitable, liberal, impartial, nonpartisan, fair-minded, unbiased, unprejudiced.

fair-minded
not biased or prejudiced; fair, just, impartial, equitable, nonjudgmental. broad-minded, reasonable, neutral.

faithful
adhering devotedly to a person, cause or duty; loyal, true, constant, firm, devoted, dedicated, patriotic, resolute, staunch, steadfast, reliable, dependable, tried and true, honest, sincere, truthful, veracious, upright, moral, virtuous, high-principled.

famous
widely known and esteemed; famed, prominent, notable, distinguished, eminent, illustrious, renowned, preeminent, celebrated, prestigious, redoubtable, legendary, acclaimed.

fanciful
displaying fancy or whimsy; whimsical, imaginative, romantic, poetic, inventive, original, creative.

fantastic
incredibly great; incredible, amazing, marvelous, fabulous, astounding, miraculous, stupendous, superb, phenomenal, wondrous.

farsighted
possessing foresight; farseeing, prudent, prescient, foresighted, wise, sagacious, discerning, acute, provident, judicious.

fascinating
possessing the power to charm or allure; magnetic, winsome, alluring, charming, appealing, enchanting, engaging, captivating, fetching, bewitching, prepossessing, sweet, entrancing, interesting, lovely, pretty, attractive.

fashionable
in accordance with the latest fashion; smart, chic, modish, dapper, stylish, jaunty, dashing, elegant, classy, well-dressed, sharp, natty, spruce, rakish.

fast
1. learning, perceiving or responding with speed; bright, intelligent, smart, clever, keen, sharp, quick-witted, quick, ingenious, acute, shrewd. **2.** moving with speed and dexterity; agile, active, brisk, facile, nimble, spry, yare, swift, fleet, speedy, lively, frisky.

fatherly
characteristic of a father; paternal, kind, beneficent, benevolent, benign, tender, affectionate, sympathetic, obliging, understanding, forbearing, protective.

fearless
having or showing courage; bold, brave, dashing, unafraid, daring, adventurous, dauntless, gutsy, intrepid, mettlesome, undaunted, heroic, gallant, chivalrous, valiant, valorous, audacious, doughty, game, plucky, lionhearted, stout-hearted, steadfast, determined, unfaltering.

fecund
marked by intellectual productivity or creativity; fertile, productive, prolific, creative, resourceful, ingenious, inventive: *a fecund mind.*

feeling
having or exhibiting compassion; sensitive, emotional, responsive, warm, tender, tender-hearted, soft, soft-hearted, caring, sympathetic, compassionate.

feisty
full of spirit or pluck; frisky, spunky, spirited, high-spirited, lively, game, mettlesome, nervy.

felicitous
appropriate for the occasion; apt, well-timed, well-suited, well-put, seemly, well-said, well-expressed, well-chosen: *a felicitous comment.*

feminine
characteristic of, or befitting a woman; womanly, ladylike, soft, delicate, gentle, tender, refined, genteel, well-bred, decorous, elegant, gracious.

fertile
marked by mental productivity; fecund, creative, ingenious, prolific, productive, resourceful: *a fertile imagination.*

fervent
afire with intense feeling; passionate, ardent, impassioned, fiery, fervid, intense, enthusiastic, keen, zealous, ablaze, animated, excited, spirited.

fetching
very pleasing to the eye or mind; sweet, lovely, pretty, attractive, magnetic, charming, fascinating, appealing, enchanting, engaging, captivating, winning, alluring, bewitching, enticing, entrancing, prepossessing.

fiery
ablaze with intense feeling; lively, eager, passionate, impassioned, ardent, fervent, fervid, aflame, afire, vibrant, high-spirited, animated.

fine
1. exceptionally good of its kind; choice great, excellent, superior, superb, prime, splendid, first-class, first-rate, capital, champion. **2.** pleasing to the eye and mind; fair, handsome, gorgeous, beautiful, pretty, lovely, attractive, comely, cute, becoming, bonny, refined, cultured, polished, tasteful, elegant, delicate, dainty, precious, exquisite.

finished
highly accomplished or polished; skilled, practiced, proficient, expert, professional, masterful, talented, gifted, adroit, deft, clever, facile, refined, elegant, graceful: *a finished dancer.*

firm
marked by determination or constancy; determined, decisive, resolute, sure, staunch, resolved, earnest, intent, serious, purposeful, thoughtful, deliberate, persevering, constant, steadfast, true, enduring, unflagging, indomitable.

first-class
of the foremost rank or highest quality; excellent, superlative, best, first-rate, supreme, extraordinary, exceptional, topnotch, crowning, greatest, unsurpassed, matchless, peerless, outstanding, remarkable.

first-rate
marked by excellence; exceptional, excellent, supreme, superlative, first-class, best, extraordinary, outstanding, remarkable.

flawless
without flaw; unmarred, unsullied, unblemished, untarnished, complete, perfect, matchless, superb: *her flawless reputation, a flawless performance.*

flexible
1. responsive to change; adaptable, resilient, versatile, cooperative, easy, amenable, agreeable, affable. **2.** able to move with ease; limber, lithe, supple, lissome, loose, nimble, agile, quick, active, light.

flourishing
improving, growing or succeeding steadily; healthy, robust, successful, thriving, booming, prospering.

fluent
speaking or writing with ease of expression; eloquent, articulate, well-spoken, smooth.

focused
marked by clarity and attention; clear, sure, intent, definite, positive, attentive, sharp, alert, keen, certain, unwavering.

forbearing
having self-control or patience; patient, tolerant, self-controlled, easy, moderate, lenient, clement, charitable, forgiving, merciful.

forgiving
inclined or able to forgive; merciful, compassionate, humane, clement, forbearing, lenient.

forthright
speaking freely and directly; open, frank, direct, straight, outspoken, candid, honest, straightforward, undisguised, free-speaking, free, plain-spoken, uninhibited.

fortunate
characterized by good fortune or luck; lucky, blessed, successful, prosperous.

frank
open and honest in expressing one's feelings or thoughts; open, direct, honest, candid, straightforward, forthright, undisguised, outspoken, uninhibited, guileless, genuine, sincere, ingenuous, aboveboard.

free
without influence or constraint; independent, autonomous, liberated, uninhibited, unreserved, natural, open, free-thinking, outspoken, ingenuous.

free-handed
marked by generosity; generous, munificent, unselfish, giving, liberal, open-handed, benevolent, charitable, beneficent, philanthropic, altruistic.

free-spoken
speaking freely and directly; open, direct, straight, honest, frank, free, candid, undisguised, plain-spoken, ingenuous, outspoken, uninhibited, straightforward.

friendly
showing friendliness or goodwill; congenial, affable, agreeable, open, amicable, amiable, amenable, good-natured, companionable, sociable, easygoing, approachable, gentle, nice, pleasant, lovable, benign, kind, charming, sweet-tempered, winning, engaging, understanding, obliging, peaceable, courteous, gracious.

frisky
marked by energy and playfulness; energetic, lively, exuberant, spirited, high-spirited, spunky, animated, active, playful, coltish, frolicsome, sportive, gay, joyful, jolly, jovial, merry, mirthful.

frolicsome
high-spirited and gay; frisky, playful, festive, merry, exuberant, animated.

frugal
prudent in the use of resources; economical, thrifty, provident, canny, temperate, moderate, conservative.

fulfilling
marked by pleasure or satisfaction; pleasing, satisfying, gratifying, rewarding..

funny
inciting laughter or amusement; humorous, amusing, comic, comical, droll, sportive, risible, zany, witty, jocose, jolly, farcical, jovial.

G

gallant
showing courage or concern for others; bold, brave, heroic, fearless, courageous, dauntless, intrepid, stout, mettlesome, lionhearted, adventurous, valiant, daring, game, dashing, doughty, plucky, courtly, chivalrous, knightly, courteous, gracious, mannerly, deferential.

game
displaying a courageous spirit; gamy, plucky, high-spirited, lionhearted, spirited, spunky, courageous, frisky, lively, mettlesome, nervy, persistent, resolute: *the game soccer team.*

gay
exhibiting joyful exuberance; merry, happy, jolly, light-hearted, blithe, festive, gleeful, jovial, mirthful, glad, joyous, cheery, bright, airy, sunny, sprightly, animated, vivacious, lively, spirited, chipper, buoyant, playful, frolicsome, convivial.

generous
liberal in giving help, money or kindness; charitable, altruistic, philanthropic, compassionate, humane, benevolent, benefic, helpful, good, kind, considerate, unselfish, sympathetic, benign, munificent, giving, magnanimous, big-hearted, good-natured, tolerant, lenient, forbearing, merciful.

genial
possessing a pleasant or friendly disposition; amiable, likable, affable, good-natured, sweet, nice, amicable, amenable, warm-hearted, winsome, engaging, appealing, charming, easy, good-humored, polite, mannerly, courteous, sociable, companionable, congenial, fraternal, approachable, open, unreserved.

genteel
characterized by good manners and refinement; polite, courteous, well-bred, mannerly, decorous, proper, thoroughbred, elegant, graceful, refined, gracious, gentle, ladylike, gentlemanly, courtly, chivalric, gallant, polished, finished, urbane, cultivated, suave, sophisticated, cosmopolitan.

gentle
having a kindly, considerate manner; soft, mild, tender, soft-hearted, kind, gracious, benign, clement, lenient, compassionate, thoughtful, amiable, affable, considerate, good-natured, sweet-tempered.

gentlemanly
having the qualities of a gentleman; courteous, well-bred, genteel, polite, courtly, gallant, manly, thoughtful, considerate, civil, accommodating, decent, decorous, elegant, refined, suave, urbane, cultivated, dignified.

genuine
free from hypocrisy or pretense; sincere, real, true, honest, truthful, veracious, unaffected, heartfelt, good, earnest, natural, artless, ingenuous, guileless, innocent, naive, simple, pure, frank, open, free, candid, plain, straightforward.

gifted
having natural ability, intelligence or talent; skillful, expert, proficient, masterful, able, capable, competent, adept, accomplished, apt, polished, adroit, deft, intelligent, ingenious, brilliant, clever, bright, quick, smart, acute, sharp, talented, endowed.

glad
expressing or feeling joy; delighted, pleased, happy, tickled, cheerful, joyful, elated, merry, jolly, jovial, gay, light-hearted, gleeful, mirthful, bright, airy, sunny, playful, sportive, frolicsome, festive, convivial.

glamorous
characterized by glamour; attractive, alluring, charming, inviting, enticing, irresistible, captivating, intriguing, fascinating, entrancing, beguiling, bewitching, enrapturing, interesting, appealing, enchanting, exciting.

gleeful
marked by joy and merriment; merry, jolly, light-hearted, blithe, happy, festive, gay, jocund, jovial, mirthful, cheery, glad, joyful, bright, sunny, airy, sprightly, animated, lively, spirited, chipper, buoyant, vivacious, overjoyed, jubilant, exuberant, effervescent, playful, frolicsome, convivial.

glorious
having extraordinary elegance, beauty or splendor; elegant, gorgeous, wonderful, superb, marvelous, sensational, sublime, magnificent, terrific, delightful, charming, captivating, enchanting, spectacular, wondrous, fabulous, awesome, heavenly, excellent, grand, splendid, resplendent.

glowing
1. aglow with joy, enthusiasm or love; aglow, beaming, shining, sunny, radiant, bright, cheerful, happy, delighted, gay, glad, gleeful, blissful, joyous, sparkling, bubbling, smiling, light-hearted, convivial, playful, winsome, mirthful, excited, enthusiastic, elated. **2.** marked by approval and favor; complimentary, favorable: *a glowing review.*

godly
faithful to the laws of God; pious, devout, devoted, religious, holy, spiritual, saintly, reverent, humble, worshipful, righteous, moral, virtuous.

good
1. characterized by kindness or honor; goodly, big, kind, humane, benevolent, altruistic, beneficent, benign, dependable, trustworthy, reliable, commendable, exemplary, virtuous, moral, honest, righteous, honorable, noble, upstanding, right, upright, wholesome, respectable, proper, decorous. **2.** marked by ability; competent, efficient, capable, proficient, adept, knowledgeable, skillful, adroit, qualified, expert, accomplished.

good-hearted
marked by a kind and generous nature; good, big, caring, humane, loving, kindly, gentle, tender, warm-hearted, chivalrous, humanitarian, altruistic, beneficent, charitable, benign, munificent, considerate, thoughtful, understanding, liberal, compassionate, clement, lenient, helpful, obliging, amicable, amiable, cordial, friendly.

good-humored
marked by a cheerful or pleasant nature; merry, gay, cheery, blithe, jolly, sunny, optimistic, convivial, genial, glad, happy, light-hearted, lively, buoyant, delightful, vivacious, enthusiastic, spirited, likable, nice, agreeable, affable, sweet, good-tempered, easygoing, engaging, appealing, charming, winning.

good-looking
possessing qualities that delight the eye; beautiful, handsome, attractive, lovely, pretty, fair, seemly, comely, bonny, gorgeous, pulchritudinous, ravishing, pleasing, appealing, glowing, blooming, wholesome, radiant, graceful, elegant.

good-natured
characterized by a kindly or pleasant disposition; kind, caring, good, big, humane, loving, gentle, benign, tender, warm-hearted, considerate, agreeable, likable, amiable, affable, cordial, genial, amenable, sweet, nice, accommodating, easygoing, appealing, charming, winning, courteous, friendly, sociable.

good-tempered
marked by a cheerful and amiable nature; merry, cheery, gay, blithe, jolly, sunny, optimistic, positive, gleeful, glad, happy, buoyant, lively, light-hearted, delightful, pleasant, enthusiastic, agreeable, affable, easygoing, likable, nice, sweet, good-humored, amenable, engaging, appealing, charming, winning.

gorgeous
1. dazzlingly beautiful; fair, lovely, pretty, attractive, handsome, good-looking, comely, pulchritudinous, ravishing. **2.** magnificent; splendid, splendiferous, dazzling, brilliant, radiant, marvelous, breathtaking, exquisite, elegant, wonderful, grand, sensational, superb, perfect, sublime.

graceful
showing grace of movement, form or manner; smooth, fluid, flowing, lithe, facile, agile, nimble, lissome, elegant, refined, cultured, polished, decorous, suave, mannerly, winning, charming, appealing, lovely, comely, attractive.

gracious
characterized by kindness, courtesy or good taste; benign, benevolent, clement, kind-hearted, gentle, warm, compassionate, friendly, amiable, sociable, pleasant, genial, congenial, cordial, well-mannered, courteous, polite, urbane, suave, polished, refined, cultured.

grand
very good or excellent; magnificent, great, glorious, splendid, superb, fine, fantastic, fabulous, first-rate, wonderful, marvelous.

grateful
feeling or showing gratitude; thankful, appreciative, pleased.

gratifying
marked by pleasure or satisfaction; pleasing, satisfying, fulfilling, rewarding.

great
exceptionally good of its kind; significant, important, paramount, illustrious, preeminent, eminent, celebrated, esteemed, notable, incomparable, matchless, sublime, magnificent, majestic, glorious, fine, splendid, superb, excellent, superior, grand, first-class, supreme.

gregarious
disposed to being sociable and talkative; outgoing, extroverted, social, affable, amicable, genial, companionable, cordial, hospitable, neighborly, friendly, warm-hearted, hearty, convivial, communicative.

guileless
free of guile; honest, ingenuous, genuine, sincere, veracious, open, innocent, aboveboard, square, honorable, decent, trustworthy, upright, upstanding, true, frank, candid, direct, straightforward, forthright, unambiguous.

gutsy
displaying courage or daring; gamy, plucky, lionhearted, spunky, brave, courageous, persistent, mettlesome, nervy, lively, spirited, uninhibited.

H

hale
having robust good health; healthy, well, hardy, sturdy, whole, sound, solid, able-bodied, energetic, hearty, fit, blooming, flourishing, fresh, vigorous, robust, strong, spirited, rugged, strapping, stalwart, brawny: *hale and hearty.*

handsome
pleasing or dignified in appearance; attractive, good-looking, beautiful, comely, fair, lovely, bonny, pretty, graceful, elegant, tasteful, aesthetic.

handy
possessing skill and ease in using the hands; adroit, dexterous, nimble, apt, deft, daedel, nimble-fingered, neat, adept, skillful, artful, quick, proficient, expert, masterly.

happy
characterized by joy or contentment; bright, light-hearted, sunny, gay, cheerful, blithe, upbeat, optimistic, positive, carefree, debonair, airy, buoyant, breezy, happy-go-lucky, easygoing, jovial, merry, jocund, mirthful, joyful, jubilant, gleeful, elated, overjoyed, delighted, glad, pleased, thrilled, tickled, content.

happy-go-lucky
without care or worry; carefree, light, cheerful, merry, jocund, jolly, gay, joyful, light-hearted, blithe, debonair, jaunty, lively, spirited, animated, sprightly.

hardy
1. marked by robust good health; hearty, healthy, able-bodied, whole, sound, well, solid, fit, energetic, vigorous, blooming, robust, rugged, sturdy, strapping, brawny, strong. **2.** capable of enduring considerable hardship; stalwart, intrepid, resolute, determined, firm, staunch, steadfast, indefatigable, unwavering, enduring, lionhearted, mettlesome, stout, courageous, valiant, brave.

harmonious
1. marked by agreement in feelings or actions; agreeable, amiable, peaceable, friendly, congenial, cordial, compatible, affectionate, loving: *a harmonious friendship.* **2.** pleasing or agreeable in sound; sweet-sounding, melodious, lyrical, pleasant, mellifluous, musical, flowing, dulcet, golden.

healing
making sound or whole; restorative, refreshing, nurturing: *healing words.*

healthy
marked by good health or sound condition; able-bodied, hardy, fit, sturdy, whole, sound, well, solid, wholesome, hearty, hale, energetic, vigorous, robust, strong, rugged, strapping, stalwart, brawny, booming, prospering, thriving.

heartwarming
causing warm, pleasant feelings; moving, inspiring, heartening, touching, uplifting, rewarding, gladdening, gratifying, satisfying, pleasing, enjoyable, agreeable.

hearty
1. warm and welcoming; genuine, sincere, real, true, honest, heartfelt, affectionate, cordial, congenial, amiable, affable, friendly: *a hearty greeting.* **2.** having good health; healthy, able-bodied, hardy, hale, sturdy, whole, sound, well, solid, energetic, vigorous, robust, strong, rugged, strapping, stalwart, brawny.

heedful
cautiously attentive; observant, mindful, watchful, awake, careful, canny, prudent, discreet, judicious, cautious, solicitous, protective, aware, conscientious, regardful, considerate, thoughtful.

helpful
providing benefit, support or aid; good, big, humane, loving, kindly, supportive, benign, benevolent, beneficent, altruistic, considerate, thoughtful, unselfish, kind-hearted, humanitarian, accommodating, understanding, obliging, merciful, compassionate, friendly, neighborly.

heroic
showing or possessing courage; bold, courageous, gallant, brave, chivalrous, dashing, adventurous, unafraid, daring, dauntless, stout, gutsy, fearless, game, mettlesome, undaunted, doughty, valiant, plucky, audacious, intrepid, resolved, unfaltering, unwavering.

high-class
of superior quality or degree; superior, superlative, first-rate, topnotch, elegant.

high-spirited
marked by joyful, unrestrained high spirits; exuberant, vivacious, vibrant, sparkling, ebullient, effervescent, fiery, energetic, lively, spirited, spunky, gamy, animated, coltish, playful, sportive, gay, joyful, jolly, merry, mirthful.

hilarious
extremely funny; hysterical, comical, uproarious, humorous, lively, risible, zany, witty, jocular, farcical, jovial.

hip
keenly aware of the latest trends or developments; savvy, clever, bright, smart, sharp, intelligent, informed, knowledgeable, wise, sagacious, canny, aware, alert, experienced, sophisticated, cosmopolitan, worldly, fashionable, stylish.

holy
deserving of or inspiring reverence; reverent, faithful, prayerful, moral, righteous, pure, chaste, innocent, saintly, religious, pious, devout, godly.

honest
truthful, trustworthy or open; veracious, genuine, sincere, real, unaffected, heartfelt, dependable, reliable, honorable, upright, decent, righteous, incorruptible, moral, principled, right-minded, ethical, just, fair, virtuous, direct, straight, candid, undisguised, forthright.

honorable
deserving of honor or respect; reputable, respectable, estimable, venerable, noble, incorruptible, honest, righteous, upstanding, upright, moral, virtuous, decent, principled, right-minded, fair, just, worthy, true, loyal, dependable, aboveboard, genuine.

hopeful
having or inspiring confidence or hope; optimistic, upbeat, positive, confident, sanguine, encouraging, heartening, cheering, gladdening, buoying, inspiring.

hospitable
treating guests with warmth and generosity; kindly, benevolent, benign, warm-hearted, friendly, warm, sociable, affable, amiable, pleasant, congenial, cordial, genial, courteous, polite, mannerly, gracious, xenodochial.

huggable
inviting an affectionate embrace; cuddly, embraceable.

human
indicative of the vulnerability or kindness of human beings; humane, sensitive, accessible, vulnerable, down-to-earth, sympathetic, kindly.

humane
marked by kindness and concern for others; charitable, benevolent, kind, benign, beneficent, humanitarian, human, understanding, considerate, good, loving, gentle, easy, gracious, patient, tender, forgiving, merciful, tolerant, compassionate, lenient, magnanimous.

humanitarian
concerned with the welfare of humanity; humane, philanthropic, altruistic, charitable, magnanimous, generous, benevolent, beneficent, helpful, big-hearted.

humble
characterized by feelings of humility; modest, unpretentious, deferential, unassuming, respectful, gracious, polite, obliging, agreeable.

humorous
inciting laughter or amusement; funny, amusing, comic, droll, lively, laughable, pleasurable, sportive, risible, zany, witty, jocose, jesting, jolly, farcical, jovial.

hysterical
extremely funny; hilarious, comical, uproarious, sidesplitting, humorous, entertaining, laughable, risible, zany.

I

ideal
most suitable or desirable; perfect, supreme, superb, best, superior, excellent, sterling, outstanding, model, exemplary, consummate.

illustrious
reputable because of achievement or character; great, famous, prominent, notable, renowned, distinguished, preeminent, eminent, celebrated, prestigious, redoubtable, estimable, admirable, laudable, commendable, respectable, honorable, creditable.

imaginative
marked by creativity or imagination; creative, inventive, resourceful, innovative, original, inspired, clever, artistic, ingenious, talented, poetic, romantic, fanciful, whimsical.

imitable
deserving of imitation; admirable, commendable, meritorious, notable, laudable, praiseworthy, superior, superb, excellent, sterling, model, outstanding, consummate, ideal.

impartial
free of bias or judgment; fair, liberal, objective, square, just, equitable, neutral, reasonable, nonjudgmental, nonpartisan, unbiased, unprejudiced, tolerant, judicious, broad-minded.

impassioned
afire with intense feeling; passionate, fervent, ardent, burning, inspired, zealous, earnest, lively, animated, alive, energetic, vivacious, dynamic, sparkling, excited, enthusiastic, eager, emotional, emotive.

imperturbable
not easily disturbed or excited; calm, serene, collected, composed, cool, together, relaxed, easygoing, cool-headed, unruffled, even-tempered, self-possessed.

important
having special value or importance; significant, meaningful, essential, vital, valuable, big, great, principal, leading, foremost, special, eminent, outstanding, prominent, notable, noteworthy, worthy, meritorious, remarkable, influential, powerful, deep, profound.

impressive
exciting a strong or vivid impression; remarkable, grand, splendid, stately, regal, persuasive, compelling, striking, stirring, moving, touching, poignant.

incisive
characterized by a keen, discerning intellect; sharp, acute, penetrating, shrewd, perceptive, astute, clever, intelligent, smart, brainy, bright, ingenious, sapient, wise, sagacious, intuitive: *John's incisive comment reflected his understanding.*

incomparable
without equal; inimitable, peerless, matchless, unequaled, nonpareil, unrivaled, unique, model, singular, rare, outstanding, excellent, superb, superior, consummate, exemplary, perfect, ideal, sterling, magnificent, extraordinary, phenomenal.

incredible
seemingly impossible to believe; amazing, astonishing, astounding, fantastic, marvelous, wonderful, fabulous, miraculous, prodigious, stupendous, phenomenal.

indefatigable
having a capacity for protracted effort; rugged, stalwart, intrepid, courageous, mettlesome, resolute, staunch, dogged, determined, firm, steadfast, indomitable, enduring, hardy, inexhaustible, unflagging, untiring: *an indefatigable worker.*

independent
free of the influence or control of others; autonomous, free-thinking, self-directed, different, liberated, individualistic, unconventional.

indispensable
absolutely essential or necessary; vital, important, irreplaceable, invaluable.

individual
possessing or showing unique or unusual qualities; individualistic, singular, distinct, different, original, unconventional, independent, special, eccentric.

indomitable
that which cannot be overcome as with persons, courage or will; firm, invincible, stalwart, persevering, doughty, determined, unswerving, resolute, indefatigable, steadfast, staunch, tireless, unflagging: *Julie's indomitable will brought her safely through the storm.*

industrious
marked by steady attention and diligence; studious, assiduous, sedulous, diligent, intent, steady, earnest, zealous, tireless, thorough, persistent, persevering, unfaltering, unswerving, indefatigable.

influential
having or exercising influence; effective, powerful, persuasive, significant, important, prestigious.

informal
not marked by formality or ceremony; casual, easygoing, relaxed, natural, unpretentious, carefree, unceremonious.

informative
serving to educate or inform; educational, enlightening, instructive.

ingenious
marked by originality or cleverness; inventive, resourceful, imaginative, original, creative, innovative, fertile, bright, intelligent, smart, brilliant, talented, sharp, agile, acute, keen, clever, quick-witted, quick, adept, apt, facile, inspired.

ingenuous
marked by candor or innocence; candid, frank, straightforward, forthright, direct, open, straight, free-spoken, aboveboard, honest, undisguised, innocent, genuine, simple, sincere, guileless: *The girl was ingenuous with us as she explained what happened.*

inimitable
cannot be imitated; matchless, peerless, incomparable, unequaled, nonpareil, unrivaled, unique, model, singular, ideal, outstanding, superb, excellent, consummate, exemplary, rare, magnificent, remarkable, extraordinary, phenomenal.

innocent
free from guile, deceit or cunning; naive, simple, natural, childlike, guileless, open, candid, ingenuous, frank, honest, unaffected, sincere, pure, chaste, virtuous, righteous, moral, decent, upright.

innovative
introducing new things or new ideas; original, creative, ingenious, inventive, imaginative, resourceful, inspired, bright, smart, intelligent, brilliant, talented, sharp, agile, keen, quick, facile, adept, clever, new, fresh, novel.

inquisitive
eager to learn; curious, inquiring, questioning, searching.

insightful
marked by insight or perception; aware, wise, knowing, sapient, sagacious, sage, discriminating, astute, sharp, keen, quick, clever, perspicacious, percipient, clear-headed, sensitive, thoughtful, sensible, reasonable, intelligent, smart, bright.

inspired
marked by inspiration; impassioned, enthused, motivated, animated, excited, enlivened, exhilarated, energized: *an inspired idea.*

inspiring
giving inspiration; exciting, thrilling, exhilarating, uplifting, stimulating, stirring, energizing, vitalizing.

instinctive
prompted by a natural tendency or impulse; intuitive, spontaneous, natural.

intellectual
using or appealing to the intellect; enlightened, well-informed, literary, lettered, learned, knowledgeable, erudite, scholarly, versed, brainy, intelligent, conversant, thoughtful, sophisticated, enlightening, informative.

intelligent
having or showing intelligence; brilliant, bright, smart, sharp, acute, alert, astute, intellectual, brainy, clever, quick-witted, ingenious, gifted, knowledgeable, scholarly, erudite, learned, wise, well-read, reasonable, logical, enlightened.

intense
marked by strong or earnest feeling; passionate, ardent, impassioned, fiery, burning, fervid, enthusiastic, zealous, animated, excited, spirited.

interesting
arousing or holding the attention of; fascinating, intriguing, stimulating, exciting, absorbing, engrossing, riveting, captivating, enchanting, inviting, charming, appealing, engaging, fetching.

intrepid
resolutely courageous; fearless, bold, brave, courageous, unafraid, dauntless, mettlesome, game, stout-hearted, heroic, gallant, valorous, daring, adventurous, confident, resolute, audacious, doughty, plucky, lionhearted, stalwart.

intuitive
perceiving through intuition; natural, instinctive, instinctual, spontaneous, perceptive, insightful, discerning.

invaluable
of great value; valuable, precious, priceless, rare, excellent, superlative, super, exceptional, extraordinary, unparalleled, inimitable, matchless, peerless, exquisite, first-rate, unique, unusual, singular, uncommon.

inventive
marked by originality or cleverness; original, imaginative, ingenious, creative, innovative, resourceful, inspired, bright, smart, intelligent, brilliant, talented, agile, acute, keen, clever, sharp-witted, quick, facile.

invigorating
able to fill with energy or strength; refreshing, stimulating, enlivening, energizing, vitalizing, strengthening.

invincible
not capable of being overcome or subdued; indomitable, stalwart, doughty, steadfast, staunch, firm, determined, resolute, persevering, indefatigable, tireless, unflagging, brave, courageous, valiant, bold, lionhearted, intrepid, daring, spirited: *invincible courage.*

irreplaceable
that cannot be replaced; invaluable, one-of-a-kind, unique, priceless, precious, vital, indispensable.

irrepressible
that cannot be repressed; exuberant, free, uninhibited, lively, vivacious, effervescent, buoyant, spirited.

irreproachable
beyond reproach; honest, moral, respectable, principled, righteous, upstanding, ethical.

irresistible
having an overpowering appeal; lovable, adorable, huggable, kissable, endearing, cuddly, magnetic, charming, fascinating, enchanting, fetching, alluring, winning, enticing, bewitching, captivating, entrancing, intriguing.

J

jaunty
1. having a self-confident, buoyant manner; airy, breezy, light-hearted, sprightly, lively, blithe, brisk, easy, cheerful, bouncy, frisky, chipper, jolly, jovial, merry, joyful, gay. **2.** being smartly attired; chic, debonair, smart, stylish, attractive, trim, neat, natty, spruce, colorful, sporty.

jazzy
lively and animated; lively, spirited, zesty, zestful, buoyant, brisk, vivacious.

jocose
characterized by joking or jesting; jocular, mischievous, playful, sportive, waggish, funny, comic, quick-witted, witty, droll, amusing, humorous, hilarious, jocund, jolly, farcical, silly.

jocular
given to joking or jesting; jocose, playful, prankish, comical, jolly, jovial, waggish, droll, entertaining.

jocund
full of fun, good cheer and high spirits; jolly, jovial, cheerful, gay, merry, light-hearted, jocose, joyous, blithe, buoyant, sunny, mirthful, gleeful, carefree, chipper, debonair, jaunty, sprightly, optimistic, happy-go-lucky, positive, breezy, airy, glad, delighted, lively, animated, vivacious, friendly, convivial.

jolly
showing or causing gaiety or good cheer; jocund, jovial, joyful, happy, cheerful, sunny, glad, blithesome, gleeful, jocular, buoyant, bubbly, exuberant, playful, frisky, coltish.

jovial
marked by hearty good humor; jolly, jocund, merry, happy, cheerful, gay, joyful, bubbly, blithe, light-hearted, mirthful, playful, jocose, vivacious, effervescent.

joyful
feeling, expressing or causing joy; joyous, glad, gay, cheerful, blithe, light-hearted, optimistic, upbeat, positive, jolly, jocund, buoyant, cheery, festive, sparkling, merry, happy, blissful, gleeful, jubilant, exultant, elated, pleased, overjoyed, heartening, heartwarming, uplifting, delightful, agreeable, pleasant.

jubilant
triumphantly joyful; triumphant, exultant, thrilled, elated, exhilarated, overjoyed, rhapsodic, euphoric, ecstatic, blissful, delighted, joyous, cheerful, gleeful, merry, beaming.

judicious
having or exhibiting prudence and good judgment; reasonable, sound, rational, sensible, sane, discerning, politic, tactful, prudent, discreet, mindful, circumspect, sage, sapient, wise, commonsensical, practical, logical, balanced, level-headed, well-grounded, enlightened, astute, aware, farsighted, knowledgeable.

just
fair and without prejudice; fair, liberal, objective, nonjudgmental, impartial, nonpartisan, equitable, square, even-handed, open-minded, unprejudiced, judicious, unbiased, tolerant, reasonable, neutral, sincere, good, honest, truthful, scrupulous, earnest, principled, moral, ethical, noble, honorable.

K

keen
1. intensely interested; enthusiastic, eager, ardent, fervent, passionate, zealous, intent, animated, avid, thirsting, ambitious, enterprising, diligent. **2.** mentally quick and original; bright, smart, intelligent, alert, aware, astute, clever, wise, sagacious, sapient, sharp-witted, sensitive, discerning, cognizant, acute, perceptive.

keen-eyed
marked by keen perception; astute, alert, acute, keen, sharp, quick, perspicacious, percipient, prudent, discriminating, discerning, cautious, vigilant, mindful, clear-headed.

keen-witted
mentally quick and original; smart, intelligent, bright, clever, aware, alert, astute, sagacious, sapient, wise, quick-witted, sharp, acute, cognizant, perceptive.

kind
marked by a tender, considerate nature; kindly, good, mild, gentle, sympathetic, compassionate, benign, benevolent, beneficent, big-hearted, loving, magnanimous, generous, charitable, decent, good-natured, helpful, obliging, affable, cordial, gracious, forgiving, lenient, clement, understanding, thoughtful, warm, accommodating, courteous, genial, amiable, neighborly.

kind-hearted
marked by kindness or sympathy; kind, big, gentle, benign, benignant, well-meaning, altruistic, charitable, warm-hearted, compassionate, amicable, sympathetic, chivalrous, merciful, understanding, thoughtful, considerate, friendly.

kingly
resembling or befitting a king; regal, royal, grand, dignified, noble, proud, assured, stately, poised, striking, commanding: *a kingly manner.*

kissable
inviting an affectionate kiss; dear, adorable, lovable, cute, precious, irresistible.

knowing
characterized by discernment or knowledge; smart, sharp, ingenious, keen, clever, astute, perceptive, deep, percipient, cognizant, sensible, discerning, wise, sagacious, sage, conversant, knowledgeable, versed, well-informed, intelligent, erudite, worldly, savvy, cultivated, cultured, enlightened: *very knowing about information technology.*

knowledgeable
having knowledge or understanding; intelligent, brilliant, intellectual, learned, scholarly, academic, well-educated, literate, well-versed, skillful, expert, proficient, erudite, cognizant, knowing, understanding, aware, discerning, insightful, wise, perceptive, sage, sapient, prudent, sensible, discreet, enlightened, cultured, worldly, sophisticated.

L

ladylike
having the qualities of a lady; feminine, delicate, gentle, tender, refined, cultured, genteel, noble, stately, dignified, womanly, elegant, well-spoken, well-bred, mannerly, proper, respectable, considerate, gracious, kind, polite, courteous.

laid-back
marked by a casual, easygoing manner; relaxed, informal, easy, agreeable, genial, unflappable, tolerant, imperturbable.

large-hearted
having a kind and generous nature; kindly, gracious, unselfish, good, loving, big-hearted, charitable, benevolent, beneficent, benign, helpful, humane, compassionate, munificent, giving, forbearing, forgiving, merciful, sympathetic, considerate, gentle, soft, tender, mild, noble, decent, honorable.

larksome
marked by mischief and playfulness; energetic, lively, playful, spirited, animated, spunky, mischievous, silly, sportive, coltish, frolicsome, gamy, mirthful: *His larksome antics amused the crowd.*

laudable
deserving of admiration; admirable, commendable, estimable, honorable, meritorious, praiseworthy, notable, creditable.

laughable
arousing laughter; humorous, funny, amusing, comical, pleasurable, droll, risible, sportive, zany, witty, jocose, jolly, jovial, hilarious, uproarious.

law-abiding
obeying the law; lawful, upstanding, upright, dutiful, good, righteous, honorable, principled.

leading
most important or principal; capital, paramount, foremost, preeminent, outstanding, cardinal, greatest, peerless, matchless, incomparable, unequaled, unsurpassed.

learned
marked by profound knowledge and scholarship; wise, sage, scholarly, knowledgeable, erudite, intelligent, intellectual, versed, well-informed, well-schooled, literate, well-read, well-versed, cultured, academic, educated, literary, accomplished, masterful, proficient, practiced, expert, skillful, profound, deep, worldly-wise, sophisticated, savvy, aware, enlightened, conversant.

lenient
characterized by understanding and tolerance; tolerant, understanding, forbearing, forgiving, charitable, clement, easygoing, magnanimous, liberal, moderate, patient, soft, mild, tender, benevolent, kind-hearted, big-hearted, humane, considerate, compassionate, sympathetic.

lettered
highly educated or learned; literate, literary, well-educated, well-versed, well-informed, enlightened, refined, cultivated, accomplished.

level-headed
showing or having good judgment or prudence; reasonable, rational, sane, sound, sensible, judicious, prudent, circumspect, balanced, commonsensical, sagacious, wise, composed, cool-headed, collected, together, self-possessed, poised, even-tempered, steady, unflappable, calm, imperturbable, unruffled.

liberal
1. favoring progress; progressive, modern, free-thinking. **2.** free from prejudice; unbiased, broad-minded, tolerant, impartial, unprejudiced. **3.** marked by generosity; charitable, beneficent, benevolent, generous, magnanimous, giving, unselfish, open-handed.

liberated
independent or non-conforming; free, emancipated, autonomous, free-thinking, self-directed, self-governed.

light
1. marked by cheerfulness; light-hearted, carefree, blithe, debonair, gay, sunny, cheery, happy, bright, happy-go-lucky, optimistic, upbeat, easygoing, breezy, merry, glad, jocund, joyful, gleeful. **2.** moving with ease; spry, supple, sprightly, nimble, agile, lithe, airy, buoyant.

light-hearted
free from anxiety or care; light, cheerful, gay, happy, positive, sunny, buoyant, blithe, carefree, happy-go-lucky.

light-footed
being light on one's feet; sprightly, spry, airy, bouncy, lightsome, lithe, buoyant, nimble, agile, swift, fleet.

lightsome
light in manner, form or movement; light, light-hearted, light-footed.

likable
easily liked; sweet, pleasant, nice, agreeable, amiable, kind, friendly, neighborly, warm, genial, congenial, good-natured, charming, winning, engaging, cute, adorable, lovable.

limber
bending or moving easily; flexible, lithe, supple, lissome, nimble, agile, quick, active, light: *the limber fireman.*

lionhearted
possessing extraordinary courage; brave, courageous, valorous, heroic, stout-hearted, gallant, bold, intrepid, dauntless, stalwart, audacious, steadfast, invincible, indomitable, unconquerable, plucky, game, spirited, spunky, fearless, gutsy.

lissome
able to move with ease; limber, lithe, lithesome, flexible, supple, nimble, agile, quick, active, light: *the lissome gymnast.*

literate
having an education or knowledge of literature; knowledgeable, versed, well-educated, well-informed, well-read, erudite, scholarly, literary.

lithe
able to move with ease; lithesome, limber, lissome, flexible, supple, nimble, agile, quick, active, light.

lively
full of life or energy; alive, dynamic, energetic, vivacious, sprightly, spry, active, bouncy, buoyant, spirited, dashing, yare, gay, jocund, breezy, peppy, chipper, effervescent, eager, animated, enthusiastic, excited.

logical
having the ability to reason validly; rational, analytical, reasonable, sound, sensible, intelligent, smart, judicious.

lovable
having a nature that attracts love or affection; adorable, cherishable, dear, endearing, precious, darling, cuddly, likable, pleasant, warm, tender, sweet, winsome, engaging, captivating, enchanting, charming.

loved
regarded with much affection and love; beloved, cherished, adored, admired, respected, esteemed, valued, treasured.

loving
feeling or showing love or affection; affectionate, tender, gentle, devoted, caring, kind, considerate, benign, thoughtful, warm-hearted, friendly, amiable, passionate, ardent.

loyal
faithful as to a person, duty or cause; true, constant, firm, steady, fast, resolute, staunch, steadfast, devoted, dedicated, dependable, reliable, supportive, dutiful, true-blue, yeomanly, patriotic, honest, trustworthy, earnest, scrupulous, sincere, veracious, straight.

lucid
easily understood; unambiguous, plain, distinct, concise, explicit, clear, sound, rational: *his lucid explanation.*

lucky
marked by luck or good fortune; fortunate, blessed, charmed, successful, prosperous.

luminous
intelligent and enlightened; bright, intellectual, gifted, brilliant, sage, discerning, perspicacious, sapient, sharp-witted, deep, penetrating, profound, inspiring, scholarly, erudite, learned: *a luminous writer.*

luscious
very appealing to the senses or mind; delightful, charming, sweet, enchanting, enjoyable, pleasing, pleasurable, pleasant, agreeable, dulcet, melodious, splendid, superb, magnificent, fine: *a luscious day in the park, a luscious piece of music.*

luxurious
characterized by luxury; sumptuous, grand, plush, pleasurable, appealing, gratifying, enjoyable, agreeable: *a luxurious day off.*

lyrical
1. able to express deep personal emotion; expressive, earnest, intent, deep, fervid, impassioned, ardent, passionate: *a lyrical poet.* **2.** marked by harmony of sound; harmonious, musical, mellifluous, melodious, dulcet, flowing, smooth, golden, sweet-sounding

M

magical
mysteriously enchanting; entrancing, bewitching, captivating, fascinating, mesmerizing, enthralling.

magnanimous
generous in giving or forgiving; big, big-hearted, unselfish, benignant, kind, benign, benevolent, charitable, humane, philanthropic, liberal, fair, just, broad-minded, tolerant, lenient, merciful, patient.

magnetic
marked by an unusual power to attract; irresistible, charismatic, attractive, charming, appealing, enchanting, captivating, engaging, bewitching, entrancing, fascinating, fetching, enthralling, mesmerizing.

magnificent
characterized by extraordinary elegance, beauty or splendor; outstanding, superb, exceptional, splendid, resplendent, glorious, grand, awesome, impressive, sublime, noble, majestic, stately, regal, august, elegant, gorgeous, handsome, graceful.

manly
characteristic of, or befitting the male sex; masculine, manful, virile, strong, powerful, husky, strapping, rugged, hale, hearty, gentlemanly, protective, kind, loving, regardful, caring, honest, gallant, courageous, brave, venturesome, indomitable, valiant, heroic, daring, lionhearted, chivalrous, game, spunky.

marvelous
arousing admiration or wonder; superb, wonderful, sensational, splendid, glorious, terrific, fantastic, incredible, astonishing, amazing, super, great, astounding, fabulous, phenomenal, miraculous, smashing, tremendous, extraordinary, divine, remarkable, breathtaking, stunning.

masculine
characteristic of, or befitting a man; manly, virile, strong, robust, rugged, brawny, athletic, stalwart, daring, brave, courageous, valiant, intrepid.

masterful
characterized by a high degree of knowledge or skill; masterly, expert, proficient, adept, accomplished, skillful, artful, gifted, talented, polished, deft, adroit, matchless, peerless, consummate, admirable, excellent, superior, topnotch.

matchless
having no equal; peerless, unrivaled, unequaled, unmatchable, nonpareil, unique, incomparable, inimitable, one-of-a-kind, consummate, perfect.

maternal
characteristic of a mother; motherly, nurturing, protective, sympathetic, warm, kind, understanding, caring, loving, tender, gentle, affectionate, devoted.

mature
having reached full development or growth; responsible, dependable, adult, independent, self-sufficient, developed, wise, sensible, sage, judicious, prudent, sophisticated, experienced, seasoned, polished, refined, knowledgeable, worldly.

meaningful
having special significance or meaning; important, significant, valuable, memorable, notable, special, profound: *a meaningful experience.*

mellifluous
smoothly or sweetly flowing; mellifluent, musical, flowing, dulcet, sweet-sounding, melodic, golden, harmonious, eloquent.

mellow
made wise and gentle by experience and age; easygoing, serene, calm, laid-back, agreeable, affable, genial, amiable, good-natured.

melodious
characterized by melody; melodic, lyrical, mellifluous, harmonious, musical, sweet-sounding, dulcet, golden, pleasant.

memorable
worthy of being remembered; notable, remarkable, unforgettable, outstanding, extraordinary, special, rare, unique, fantastic, marvelous, sensational, powerful, eloquent.

merciful
of a lenient or forgiving nature; kind, compassionate, humane, tender, benign, gentle, beneficent, charitable, tolerant, forbearing, clement, soft-hearted, temperate, magnanimous, liberal.

meritorious
deserving of admiration or reward; admirable, commendable, estimable, laudable, deserving, praiseworthy, reputable, respectable, honorable, virtuous, righteous, just, principled, upright, excellent, exemplary, noble.

merry
marked by joyful exuberance; gay, jolly, light-hearted, blithe, gleeful, jocund, jovial, mirthful, festive, happy, joyous, cheery, buoyant, debonair, carefree, breezy, airy, easygoing, genial, good-natured, convivial, amiable, friendly, blissful, elated, thrilled, lively, chipper, jaunty, vivacious, sprightly.

mesmerizing
able to compel the attention or imagination of; captivating, riveting, fascinating, enthralling, spellbinding, enchanting, entrancing, bewitching.

methodical
characterized by orderly habits or behaviors; efficient, systematic, businesslike, meticulous, tidy, neat.

meticulous
marked by attentiveness to details; careful, precise, accurate, particular, conscientious, detailed, thorough, scrupulous, methodical.

mettlesome
possessing courage and spirit; bold, courageous, brave, fearless, daring, game, adventurous, dauntless, stout, valiant, gallant, heroic, plucky, gutsy, intrepid, doughty, steadfast, determined, unwavering, spirited, lionhearted, energetic, vigorous, lively, zealous, fervent, enthusiastic: *the mettlesome climber.*

mighty
marked by great strength, power or ability; strong, powerful, sturdy, hale, rugged, hardy, robust, hearty, stalwart, strapping, husky, burly, masterful, puissant, commanding, indomitable, irresistible, invincible, big, profound, superior, important.

mindful
careful and attentive; aware, awake, attentive, alert, sharp, cognizant, astute, wise, sensible, circumspect, prudent, observant, thoughtful, regardful, considerate, respectful.

miraculous
affecting great wonder or surprise; amazing, astonishing, fantastic, astounding, incredible, remarkable, stupendous, marvelous, surprising.

mirthful
marked by gaiety or merriment; merry, gay, jolly, light-hearted, blithe, gleeful, blissful, joyous, jocund, jovial, cheerful, sunny, lightsome, buoyant, optimistic, upbeat, glad, animated, vivacious, lively, chipper, jaunty, sprightly, debonair, carefree, breezy, airy, happy-go-lucky, convivial, friendly.

mischievous
full of mischief; playful, impish, elfish, devilish, sportive, coltish, frolicsome, waggish, gamesome, fun-loving, high-spirited, frisky, amusing, funny.

modern
up-to-date in style or thinking; new, hip, fashionable, popular, trendy, contemporary, liberal, avant-garde, advanced, progressive, novel.

modest
free from vanity or boastfulness; unpretentious, unassuming, humble, decorous, proper, seemly, demure.

moral
virtuous or good in character or behavior; just, fair, upright, honest, honorable, ethical, righteous, noble, decent, principled, chaste, innocent, proper, pure, decorous, responsible.

motherly
characteristic of a mother; maternal, nurturing, protective, solicitous, kind, caring, considerate, loving, affectionate, devoted, gentle, tender.

motivated
moved to take action through inspiration or resolution; ambitious, industrious, enthusiastic, energetic, inspired, impassioned, zealous, avid, dynamic, earnest, eager, resolute.

motivational
moving to effort or action; inspiring, inspirational, exciting, thrilling, exhilarating, uplifting, stimulating, stirring, energizing, vitalizing.

moving
affecting or stirring the emotions; stirring, touching, striking, thrilling, breathtaking, inspiring, effective, impressive, poignant, tender.

multidimensional
having many characteristics and dimensions; multifaceted, diverse, versatile, multifarious.

multifaceted
having many characteristics and abilities; multidimensional, diverse, versatile, resourceful, multitalented.

multitalented
having many talents and abilities; multifaceted, diverse, versatile, clever, resourceful, ingenious.

munificent
characterized by great generosity; generous, liberal, magnanimous, unsparing, bountiful, big-hearted, hospitable, beneficent, unselfish, charitable, altruistic, public-spirited, philanthropic, humanitarian: *the family's munificent donation.*

muscular
having well-developed muscles; sturdy, burly, sinewy, strapping, brawny, robust, stalwart, rugged, husky, solid, strong, athletic, well-built, able-bodied.

musical
1. skillful in music; talented, gifted, endowed, skillful, artistic. **2.** marked by harmony of sound; harmonious, mellifluous, melodious, lyrical, dulcet, smooth, golden.

mysterious
arousing wonder and inquisitiveness; enchanting, fascinating, captivating, entrancing, appealing, beguiling, alluring, enticing, engaging: *a mysterious smile.*

N

naive
characterized by natural simplicity of nature; innocent, unaffected, childlike, natural, guileless, simple, ingenuous, frank, straightforward, candid, forthright, unambiguous, open, trusting, genuine, sincere.

natty
neat, trim and smart in appearance or dress; dapper, spiffy, sharp, sleek, well-groomed, well-dressed, classy, elegant, chic, fashionable, stylish.

natural
1. having innate abilities and talents; talented, gifted, endowed. **2.** free from affectation or inhibitions; unaffected, simple, innocent, naive, ingenuous, guileless, genuine, real, authentic, spontaneous, uninhibited, free, intuitive, open, plain-spoken, candid, straightforward, informal, unpretentious, unassuming.

neat
1. orderly and clean; well-ordered, tidy, trim, well-groomed, clean-cut, smart, sleek, natty. **2.** marked by skill or cleverness; adroit, skillful, deft, daedal, adept, apt, dexterous, clever, ingenious, resourceful.

neighborly
characteristic of a good neighbor; friendly, congenial, amiable, affable, agreeable, warm-hearted, convivial, sociable, cordial, accessible, sharing, generous, hospitable, kindly, well-disposed, considerate, thoughtful, helpful, obliging, gracious, polite, courteous, peaceful.

new
known, seen or thought of for the first time; original, fresh, novel, unique, innovative, imaginative, inventive, creative, authentic, different, modern, avant-garde, advanced, revolutionary.

nice
1. having agreeable or pleasant qualities; winsome, likable, cheerful, delightful, pleasant, genial, amiable, amusing, humorous, congenial, kind, charming, gracious, friendly, warm, considerate, generous, benignant, compassionate, understanding. **2.** well-bred or respectable; decent, comely, becoming, seemly, virtuous, decorous, modest, proper, refined, cultivated, cultured.

nifty
first-rate; smart, stylish, dandy, fine.

nimble
mentally or physically adept; clever, facile, alert, awake, keen, sharp, smart, intelligent, energetic, chipper, vivacious, animated, handy, daedel, adroit, dexterous, active, agile, spry, lithe, sprightly, lively, fleet, speedy.

nimble-fingered
physically adept in using one's hands; adroit, deft, dexterous, daedel, handy, well-coordinated, facile, expert, skillful, proficient.

nimble-witted
mentally adept; clever, facile, alert, awake, sharp, wide-awake, keen, intelligent, smart, brainy, bright, quick-witted, witty, sparkling.

noble
possessing greatness of character or superior merit; moral, honorable, scrupulous, virtuous, principled, ethical, admirable, reputable, decent, magnanimous, righteous, good, just, fair, upright, worthy, veracious, honest, truthful, forthright, faithful, incorruptible, loyal: *a noble effort, noble sentiments.*

nonjudgmental
free of bias or judgment; fair, liberal, objective, square, equitable, just, fair-minded, nonpartisan, neutral, judicious, impartial, even-handed, unprejudiced, reasonable.

nonviolent
refraining from violence in favor of peace; peaceable, peace-loving, pacific, diplomatic, neutral, gentle, mild-mannered, even-tempered, easygoing, temperate, agreeable, cooperative, amicable, forbearing, patient, compassionate, clement, merciful, lenient, forgiving.

notable
1. widely known and esteemed; great, prominent, famous, eminent, illustrious, renowned, distinguished, preeminent, celebrated, noted, redoubtable, honored, prestigious, acclaimed. **2.** worthy of notice; noteworthy, memorable, special, meaningful, remarkable, significant, momentous, outstanding.

noted
widely known and esteemed; great, prominent, notable, eminent, famed, illustrious, renowned, preeminent, distinguished, celebrated, acclaimed, prestigious, redoubtable.

noteworthy
deserving of notice or attention; notable, outstanding, memorable, meaningful, remarkable, significant, unforgettable, special, momentous, extraordinary.

novel
unusual and new; original, unique, innovative, imaginative, creative, inventive, authentic, modern, unconventional, advanced, avant-garde, revolutionary, fresh, bright, clever.

nurturing
promoting and sustaining the development of; maternal, paternal, supportive, helpful, encouraging, cherishing, strengthening

O

obeisant
showing great respect; deferential, deferent, courteous, respectful, honoring: *Kathi's obeisant manner showed respect for her host's cultural differences.*

objective
not influenced by personal opinions or feelings; fair, liberal, square, just, equitable, impartial, open-minded, neutral, unbiased, unprejudiced, nonpartisan.

obliging
ready to be of service or to do favors for others; helpful, agreeable, willing, eager, amenable, gracious, accommodating, kind, friendly, neighborly, well-disposed.

observant
quick to perceive or notice; aware, alert, observing, thoughtful, mindful, heedful, watchful, attentive, intent, keen, sensitive, wide-awake, sharp.

one-and-only
without equal or rival; inimitable, incomparable, unique, peerless, matchless, unequaled, nonpareil, unrivaled, individual, one-of-a-kind.

open
1. speaking freely and sincerely; candid frank, outspoken, direct, straight, honest, straightforward, forthright, undisguised, sincere, plain-spoken. **2.** willing and ready to receive new ideas, facts or views; responsive, amenable, available, receptive, open-minded, broad-minded, unprejudiced, unbiased, impartial.

open-eyed
very attentive; alert, vigilant, eagle-eyed, wakeful, observant, watchful, awake, cognizant, attentive, heedful.

open-handed
characterized by generosity; giving, generous, unselfish, magnanimous, liberal, big-hearted, munificent, free-handed, humanitarian, unsparing, altruistic, benevolent, philanthropic.

open-hearted
1. marked by candor; frank, candid, forthright, straightforward, honest, sincere, ingenuous, natural, genuine, guileless, innocent, unreserved. **2.** generous; giving, kind-hearted, magnanimous, gentle, benevolent, benign, humane, compassionate, loving, good, warm, sympathetic.

open-minded
receptive to new ideas, facts or views; broad-minded, responsive, amenable, receptive, unprejudiced, open, unbiased, impartial, liberal, tolerant, reasonable, understanding, fair, just, sympathetic, enlightened, progressive.

optimistic
looking on the bright side of things; hopeful, sanguine, confident, cheery, positive, upbeat, cheerful, buoyant, light-hearted, blithe, sunny, carefree.

orderly
marked by good order or constancy; neat, tidy, trim, balanced, constant, steady, well-balanced, systematic, methodical, businesslike, efficient, precise, thorough, careful, attentive, alert, sharp, keen, clear-headed, level-headed.

organized
performing effectively with order and efficiency; effective, efficient, methodical, orderly, systematic, steady, businesslike, precise, sharp, clear-headed, attentive, careful, thorough, well-prepared.

original
characterized by newness, creativity or inventiveness; new, fresh, novel, unique, singular, special, different, rare, uncommon, extraordinary, creative, ingenious, imaginative, resourceful, inventive, innovative, unconventional.

outgoing
disposed to being open, sociable and talkative; responsive, unreserved, easy, amicable, genial, hospitable, cordial, friendly, neighborly, warm, convivial, amiable, approachable, affable, gregarious, extroverted, communicative, demonstrative.

outrageous
extremely unconventional or unusual; extraordinary, remarkable, singular, new, unique, novel, rare, original, uncommon, offbeat, camp.

outspoken
frank or open in speech; candid, forthright, direct, straightforward, unambiguous, explicit, undisguised, vocal, free-spoken, uninhibited.

outstanding
far above others in excellence or quality; magnificent, exceptional, remarkable, extraordinary, stunning, impressive, excellent, great, superb, splendid, terrific, sensational, first-class, marvelous, smashing, special, unforgettable, memorable.

P

pacific
characterized by a peaceful nature; peaceful, peaceable, nonviolent, placid, gentle, easygoing, agreeable, amicable, mild-mannered, tranquil, calm, serene.

palmary
deserving of the palm of victory; praiseworthy, outstanding, great, notable, memorable, meaningful, remarkable, unforgettable, special, noteworthy, momentous: *a palmary achievement.*

paramount
above all others, as in importance or influence; outstanding, preeminent, cardinal, foremost, capital, leading, important, significant, superlative, premier, supreme, incomparable, inimitable, matchless, unrivaled, champion, splendid, terrific, superb.

par excellence
being an example of excellence; superior, preeminent, superlative, incomparable, champion, prize, sterling, splendid, terrific, best, model, superb, choice, capital, prime, exceptional, outstanding, first-rate, admirable, estimable, notable, eminent, remarkable, distinguished: *His skating was par excellence and worthy of the gold.*

passionate
marked by intense or strong feelings; ardent, fervent, fervid, impassioned, amorous, burning, fiery, intense, zealous, earnest, eager, excited, enthusiastic, animated, sparkling, vivacious, lively, inspired, energetic, vital, vigorous, dynamic.

paternal
characteristic of a father; fatherly, kind, kind-hearted, nurturing, caring, loving, devoted, vigilant, protective, regardful.

patient
showing calm endurance with hardship, difficulty or provocation; persevering, constant, enduring, steady, composed, contained, cool, calm, together, even-tempered, self-possessed, philosophical, agreeable, cooperative, amenable, balanced, poised, easygoing, understanding, tolerant, forbearing, unflappable, unruffled, imperturbable.

patriotic
feeling, showing or inspired by love for one's country; nationalistic, loyal, allegiant, public-spirited.

peaceful
1. inclined or disposed to peace; peaceable, pacific, nonviolent, even-tempered, neutral, good-natured, gentle, mild-mannered, amiable, easygoing, temperate, amicable, agreeable, congenial, cooperative, placid, genial, friendly, pleasant, patient, clement, forbearing, lenient. **2.** tranquil; calm, restful, serene, relaxing, quiet.

penetrating
displaying keen insight; penetrative, perceptive, acute, sharp, shrewd, incisive, discriminating, cognizant, aware, keen, quick, intelligent.

peppy
marked by energy and high spirits; energetic, lively, active, vigorous, dynamic, brisk, spry, alive, snappy, zippy, eager, spirited, vibrant, chipper, ebullient, irrepressible, effervescent.

perceptive
having or displaying keen, discerning intellect; percipient, perspicacious, smart, intelligent, quick-witted, astute, sharp, acute, penetrating, shrewd, incisive, sensitive, cognizant, insightful, aware, discriminating, knowing, wise, sagacious, sapient.

percipient
having perception; discriminating, perceptive, perspicacious, insightful, discerning, knowing, sagacious, sage, prudent, discreet, politic, tactful, intelligent, sharp, alert, open-eyed.

perfect
1. excellent beyond improvement; whole, good, complete, exemplary, ideal, inimitable, incomparable, unsurpassed, unrivaled, matchless, superlative, supreme, superb, fine, extraordinary, exquisite, priceless, best, champion, admirable, laudable, commendable, flawless, precious, pure. **2.** thoroughly skilled; expert, masterful, skillful, efficient, gifted, proficient, talented, accomplished, experienced.

perky
marked by liveliness and vigor; brisk, jaunty, sprightly, energetic, lively, chipper, active, dynamic, spirited, peppy, frisky, frolicsome, enthusiastic, excited, vivacious, gay, bouncy, aglow, bright, sunny, blithe, buoyant, optimistic, upbeat, cheery, carefree, light-hearted, easygoing, debonair, breezy, happy-go-lucky.

persevering
remaining constant in a course of purpose or action in spite of obstacles or discouragement; constant, purposeful, patient, enduring, persistent, diligent, zealous, ambitious, industrious, sedulous, assiduous, indefatigable, indomitable, untiring, unflagging, resolute, steadfast, determined, firm, stalwart, unshakable, unwavering.

personable
pleasing in appearance or personality; attractive, handsome, good-looking, comely, agreeable, friendly, easygoing, gregarious, outgoing, companionable, sociable, amiable, likable, pleasant, good-natured, cordial, amicable, affable.

perspicacious
possessing keen powers of judgment and observation; perceptive, astute, discerning, percipient, knowing, aware, acute, keen, alert, shrewd, sharp-witted, quick, smart, bright, brainy, wise, sapient, sagacious, judicious, farsighted, sensitive, prudent: *Garth's perspicacious judgment helped his client resolve her anxiety.*

persuasive
possessing the power to persuade; impressive, effective, efficacious, satisfying, convincing, compelling.

phenomenal
so remarkable as to illicit amazement; wonderful, incredible, amazing, fantastic, extraordinary, marvelous, astonishing, fabulous, remarkable, astounding, miraculous, prodigious, unbelievable, stunning, stupendous, wondrous.

philanthropic
marked by a concern for charity and the welfare of others; charitable, benevolent, altruistic, beneficent, benign, munificent, magnanimous, generous, liberal, giving, open-handed, unsparing, public-spirited, humane, unselfish, helpful, gracious, kindly, big-hearted, compassionate.

philosophical
accepting life and it's problems with understanding and calmness; poised, level-headed, reasonable, composed, cool, collected, calm, balanced, self-possessed, practical, imperturbable, unruffled, placid, serene, tranquil.

photogenic
attractive as a subject for photography; photographic.

pious
characterized by religious reverence; religious, holy, devout, worshipful, devoted, spiritual, godly, saintly, humble, reverent, righteous, moral, virtuous.

pixyish
playfully mischievous; impish, elfish, devilish.

placid
not easily disturbed or excited; calm, collected, cool, composed, tranquil, serene, temperate, level-headed, even-tempered, self-possessed.

plain-spoken
speaking freely and sincerely; open, direct, plain, straight, truthful, frank, straightforward, forthright, candid, honest, free-speaking, uninhibited, guileless, genuine, sincere.

playful
full of fun, high spirits and humor; frolicsome, sportive, mischievous, impish, devilish, gamesome, fun-loving, waggish, high-spirited, frisky, coltish, amusing, funny, witty, jocular.

pleasant
characterized by pleasing manners or behaviors; agreeable, affable, amiable, delightful, cheery, merry, well-mannered, courteous, polite, gracious, gentlemanly, ladylike, hospitable, open, easy, nice, likable, congenial, outgoing, lively, sociable, companionable, gregarious, friendly, neighborly, charming, engaging, inviting, winning.

pleasing
giving pleasure or enjoyment; pleasant, pleasurable, agreeable, enjoyable, harmonious, delightful, gratifying, satisfying, refreshing, gay, cheerful, joyful, festive, good, nice, handsome, attractive, lovely, beautiful, elegant, prepossessing, enchanting, fascinating.

pleasurable
giving pleasure; pleasant, pleasing, agreeable, enjoyable, delightful, satisfying, gratifying, felicitous, refreshing, cheerful, joyful, festive, captivating, fascinating, bewitching.

plentiful
marked by abundance; plenteous, abundant, bountiful, rich, thriving, fertile, fecund, productive, prolific.

plucky
showing courage and spirit; bold, brave, heroic, fearless, gallant, courageous, dauntless, intrepid, stout, mettlesome, dashing, valiant, daring, valorous, lionhearted, game, doughty, audacious, spirited, gutsy, spunky, adventurous, firm, resolute, determined, steadfast, staunch, stalwart, indomitable, invincible.

poetic
having the characteristics of poetry; lyrical, musical, melodious, artistic, aesthetic, beautiful, sensuous, flowing.

poignant
stimulating deep emotions; moving, touching, stirring, soul-stirring, sensitive, tender, emotional: *a poignant article.*

poised
characterized by a calm, confident manner; composed, self-possessed, collected, imperturbable, together, cool-headed, even-tempered, placid, easygoing, serene, balanced, steady.

polished
characterized by discriminating taste and knowledge; cultivated, cultured, well-bred, civilized, enlightened, refined, urbane, educated, finished.

polite
characterized by good manners and consideration for others; respectful, deferential, decorous, proper, well-bred, tactful, politic, diplomatic, refined, ladylike, well-behaved, kind, mannerly, courteous, cordial, genial, affable, pleasant, sociable, winning, charming, ingratiating, obliging, agreeable, attentive, gracious, urbane, gallant, gentlemanly.

politic
marked by good judgment or tact; wise, knowing, sapient, sagacious, sage, discriminating, discerning, selective, astute, acute, perceptive, perspicacious, percipient, keen, sharp, judicious, sensitive, discreet, prudent, cautious, mindful, sensible, thoughtful, reasonable, sound, bright, smart, intelligent, quick.

popular
widely liked, admired or favored; well-liked, loved, beloved, famous, renowned, well-known, acclaimed, big, celebrated.

positive
having or inspiring confidence or certainty; confident, optimistic, sunny, sanguine, hopeful, sure, certain, assured, definite, secure, decisive, encouraging, affirming, inspiring, heartening, cheering, comforting.

potent
marked by effectiveness, strength or power; strong, powerful, mighty, puissant, intense, great.

powerful
1. having great strength; strong, husky, big, burly, hardy, muscular, able-bodied, hearty, strapping, sturdy, doughty, stalwart, rugged. **2.** characterized by great authority or influence; mighty, potent, puissant, dynamic, impressive, effective, eloquent, moving, persuasive, influential, prestigious, eminent, important, significant.

practical
having or showing good sense or good judgment; sensible, realistic, down-to-earth, level-headed, wise, sagacious, sage, judicious, prudent, politic, sharp, astute, efficient, effective, businesslike.

practiced
proficient as a result of study and practice; professional, accomplished, experienced, seasoned, skilled, expert, masterful, adept, talented, endowed, gifted, apt, clever, facile, suave, sophisticated, cultured, refined, learned, versed, educated.

praiseworthy
deserving of admiration; admirable, worthy, commendable, virtuous, estimable, meritorious, creditable, laudable, deserving, reputable, good, noble, righteous, respectable, honorable, excellent, exemplary.

precious
loved dearly; dear, darling, beloved, cherished, admired, valued, prized, respected, treasured, esteemed.

precise
very definite or accurate; explicit, unambiguous, positive, distinct, clear, plain.

precocious
characterized by unusually early maturity or development; smart, clever, bright, brilliant, intelligent, brainy, gifted, quick, progressive, forward, advanced.

preeminent
superior to or above all others; peerless, matchless, incomparable, inimitable, unsurpassed, unequaled, supreme, top, foremost, crowning, paramount, prominent, eminent, leading, famous, notable, illustrious, renowned, distinguished, celebrated, prestigious, redoubtable, exalted, well-known, acclaimed.

prepossessing
making a favorable impression; attractive, handsome, beautiful, lovely, agreeable, likable, pleasing, pleasant, charming, fascinating, appealing, engaging, interesting, captivating, beguiling, mesmerizing, winning, bewitching, entrancing.

prestigious
widely known and esteemed; prominent, famed, famous, great, notable, illustrious, eminent, well-known, acclaimed, renowned, exalted, preeminent, celebrated, distinguished, redoubtable.

prime
of the foremost rank or highest quality; great, fine, excellent, first-rate, superior, splendid, champion, topflight, supreme, superlative, best, exceptional, highest, crowning, greatest, unparalleled, matchless, peerless, admirable, remarkable, outstanding, estimable, meritorious.

princely
1. resembling or befitting a prince; regal, grand, royal, noble, dignified, stately, magnificent, impressive, majestic, superb, sublime. **2.** greatly liberal; generous, magnanimous, munificent, beneficent, bounteous.

principled
characterized by moral or ethical principles; just, good, fair, upright, right-minded, decent, honorable, honest, righteous, noble, virtuous, seemly, decorous, responsible.

proactive
responding to new or difficult situations effectively and positively; resourceful, ingenious, inventive, creative, sharp, quick-witted, keen, astute, capable, effective, proficient, positive, confident, assured, sure, certain, definite, decisive, optimistic: *Her proactive response to the crisis kept the group focused on solution.*

prodigious
so remarkable as to elicit disbelief; incredible, amazing, astonishing, fantastic, marvelous, phenomenal, miraculous, fabulous, stupendous, astounding, wondrous, remarkable.

productive
marked by positive, useful or abundant results; effective, efficient, constructive, fruitful, valuable, creative, inventive, imaginative, fertile, prolific: *a productive meeting, a productive writer.*

professional
possessing a high degree of skill or expertise; master, proficient, adept, masterful, skillful, expert, practiced, experienced, deft, dexterous, facile, well-informed, knowledgeable, efficient, competent, capable, thorough, conscientious.

proficient
highly skilled; expert, effective, efficient, productive, masterly, adept, apt, good, able, competent, capable, skillful, qualified, polished, finished, accomplished, versed, talented, first-rate, topnotch.

profound
1. characterized by great insight or knowledge; sagacious, wise, sage, intellectual, scholarly, well-versed, well-read, erudite, knowledgeable, learned. **2.** intensely felt; intense, penetrating, moving, soul-stirring, heart-swelling, poignant. **3.** having special value or importance; vital, important, significant, meaningful.

progressive
marked by progress, improvement or reform; modern, new, liberal, tolerant, broad-minded, forward, open-minded, precocious, advanced, avant-garde, enlightened.

prolific
producing abundantly through artistic or creative efforts; fruitful, productive, fertile, fecund.

prominent
widely known and esteemed; great, famous, notable, distinguished, eminent, illustrious, renowned, preeminent, celebrated, grand, important, acclaimed, leading, popular, remarkable, extraordinary, unforgettable, estimable, noble, honorable, exalted, respected.

prompt
marked by punctuality or readiness; punctual, timely, ready, quick.

prosperous
having wealth, good fortune or success; flourishing, thriving, wealthy, affluent, rich, abundant, fortunate, successful.

provident
1. showing forethought; farsighted, judicious, sagacious, thoughtful, wise, foresighted, ready, prepared: *provident planning.* **2.** prudent in the use of resources; economical, thrifty, canny, prudent, sparing, frugal, temperate, conservative, moderate, careful.

prudent
possessing or showing good judgment and prudence; reasonable, sound, wise, sensible, judicious, balanced, sane, commonsensical, sapient, sagacious, cautious, politic, circumspect, discerning, discreet, moderate, practical, economical, thrifty, frugal, provident.

public-spirited
exhibiting devotion to the public welfare; altruistic, philanthropic, charitable, beneficent, humanitarian, human, kind, big-hearted, princely, liberal, munificent, magnanimous.

puissant
marked by effectiveness, strength or power; strong, powerful, mighty, potent, intense, great.

pulchritudinous
having qualities that delight the eye; fair, beautiful, pretty, handsome, lovely, comely, good-looking, attractive, gorgeous, beauteous, ravishing, bonny, glowing, elegant, graceful, winsome, pleasant, engaging, charming, fetching.

punctual
arriving at the appointed time; prompt, timely, ready, constant, steady.

pure
beyond moral reproach; virtuous, good, modest, innocent, chaste, wholesome, decent, righteous, reputable, creditable, upright, honorable, moral, honest.

purposeful
having or showing determination; determined, decisive, positive, sure, committed, resolute, firm, steadfast, staunch, persevering, assiduous, diligent, sedulous, industrious, indefatigable, tireless, intent, avid, enthusiastic, energetic, zealous.

Q

quaint
pleasingly curious in an unusual way; unusual, unique, uncommon, unconventional, singular, funny, eccentric, humorous, whimsical, fanciful: *a quaint sense of humor.*

qualified
having the abilities or requirements to perform well; able, competent, skillful, efficient, effective, capable, proficient, masterful, experienced, knowledgeable, learned, trained, well-informed, prepared.

queenly
resembling or befitting a queen; regal, royal, grand, dignified, stately, noble, proud, assured, commanding, poised, striking: *a queenly bearing.*

questioning
eager to acquire knowledge; curious, inquisitive, inquiring, searching: *a questioning mind.*

quick
1. learning, perceiving or responding with speed; bright, intelligent, smart, clever, ingenious, keen, sharp, fast, quick-witted, acute, shrewd. **2.** moving with speed and dexterity; active, brisk, agile, facile, spry, nimble, yare, swift, fleet, speedy, sprightly, lively, frisky.

quick-witted
mentally alert and sharp; keen, acute, astute, bright, intelligent, smart, clever, quick, perspicacious, discerning, shrewd, penetrating, brainy, brilliant, sharp-witted, ingenious, witty, jocose.

quiescent
in a state of rest; quiet, calm, still, reposeful, untroubled, undisturbed: *a quiescent frame of mind.*

quiet
free of turmoil and agitation; calm, composed, tranquil, serene, sedate, placid, peaceable, pacific, peaceful, unruffled, undisturbed.

R

radiant
beaming with joy, contentment or love; aglow, sunny, bright, cheery, happy, delighted, glad, gay, gleeful, blissful, joyful, glowing, sparkling, shining, bubbling, winsome, smiling, convivial, light-hearted, animated, playful, enthusiastic, excited, elated.

rakish
dashingly or sportingly stylish; jaunty, smart, dapper, dashing, spruce, natty, sharp, well-groomed, handsome, debonair, classy, fine, chic, fashionable.

rapturous
showing or feeling great happiness, delight or joy; ecstatic, exhilarated, excited, thrilled, elated, enraptured, entranced, enchanted, captivated, blissful, euphoric, rhapsodic.

rare
unusually fine or valuable; unusual, singular, unique, individual, notable, distinctive, extraordinary, exquisite, remarkable, exceptional, wonderful, marvelous, preeminent, precious, superior, first-class, choice, select, invaluable, inimitable, matchless.

rational
characterized by the ability to reason; reasonable, sensible, sane, sound, wise, sapient, judicious, prudent, commonsensical, level-headed, balanced, lucid, logical, practical, clearheaded, fair, just, enlightened, perceptive, farsighted.

ravishing
extremely attractive or enchanting; beautiful, fair, lovely, handsome, pretty, gorgeous, good-looking, comely, pulchritudinous, dazzling, entrancing, bewitching, engaging, captivating, enthralling, alluring, enticing, charming, intriguing.

ready
1. mentally prepared; astute, sharp, acute, attentive, alert, perceptive, nimble-witted, bright, agile, deft, clever, shrewd, ingenious. **2.** willing; agreeable, game, keen, eager, happy, glad, enthusiastic, genial, well-disposed.

real
free from hypocrisy or pretense; honest, genuine, sincere, hearty, unaffected, heartfelt, earnest, natural, authentic, ingenuous, artless, guileless, innocent, naive, simple, pure, truthful, veracious, frank, open, free, candid, plain.

realistic
concerned with what is actual or practical; level-headed, sensible, efficient, effective, down-to-earth, businesslike.

reasonable
showing or possessing good judgment; rational, sound, sensible, sane, prudent, sagacious, wise, sage, commonsensical, balanced, well-grounded, logical, practical, lucid, discreet, just, politic, perspicacious, foresighted, thoughtful, reflective, responsible, intelligent.

receptive
willing and able to receive new ideas, views or suggestions; open, responsive, amenable, approachable, welcoming, open-minded, tolerant, broad-minded.

red-blooded
full of vitality; strong, spirited, vital, vigorous, robust.

redoubtable
commanding respect or reverence; respected, renowned, venerable, great, famous, prominent, notable, eminent, illustrious, distinguished, preeminent, celebrated, prestigious, noted: *the redoubtable soccer team.*

refined
marked by elegance and culture; cultured, civilized, cultivated, well-bred, enlightened, urbane, genteel, gentlemanly, ladylike, mannerly, polite, courtly, graceful, aesthetic, exquisite, delicate, noble, elevated, high-minded.

reflective
marked by careful or serious thinking; rational, reasonable, sensible, logical, practical, intelligent, percipient, analytic.

refreshing
stimulating mental, physical or emotional vigor; invigorating, renewing, energizing, rejuvenating, revitalizing, enlivening, exhilarating, strengthening, encouraging.

regal
befitting or resembling a king or queen; noble, dignified, proud, distinguished, grand, splendid, stately, magnificent, impressive, superb, awesome, kingly, queenly, princely: *a regal manner.*

regardful
mindful or respectful of others; deferential, attentive, heedful, aware, observant, circumspect, prudent, thoughtful, considerate, conscientious, courteous.

relaxed
not constrained by rigid standards; calm, serene, tranquil, peaceful, placid, even-tempered, collected, carefree, easygoing, informal, laid-back, casual, mild, mellow.

relaxing
affording relaxation; peaceful, quiet, restful, undisturbed, serene, tranquil.

reliable
capable of being depended upon with confidence; trustworthy, responsible, dependable, honest, upstanding, honorable, principled, conscientious, steady, firm, faithful, true, solid, steadfast, devoted, real, authentic, genuine, well-grounded, established, reputable, stable, sound.

religious
marked by devotion to religion or duty; devout, holy, pious, reverent, saintly, prayerful, spiritual, faithful, true, loyal, constant, devoted.

remarkable
marked by unusual qualities; rare, singular, exceptional, unequaled, matchless, inimitable, distinct, unique, striking, impressive, grand, outstanding, majestic, dignified, august, awesome, wondrous, best, superb, marvelous, prodigious, stupendous, amazing, astonishing, incredible, miraculous, splendid, magnificent, preeminent, superior, excellent, notable, memorable.

renowned
widely known and esteemed; great, prominent, eminent, distinguished, illustrious, notable, well-known, famous, preeminent, prestigious, redoubtable, celebrated, acclaimed, honorable, venerable, estimable, matchless, legendary, memorable.

reputable
having a good reputation; estimable, honorable, respectable, creditable, conscientious, dependable, honest, trustworthy, aboveboard, straight, irreproachable, upright, good, virtuous, scrupulous, principled.

resilient
having the ability to recover readily; irrepressible, buoyant, adaptable, flexible, lively, light-hearted, airy, perky, carefree.

resolute
marked by strong determination; purposeful, indefatigable, staunch, determined, persevering, steadfast, devoted, earnest, serious, true, constant, steady, loyal, faithful, confident, self-assured.

resourceful
having the ability or skill to deal with new or difficult situations effectively; ingenious, inventive, creative, intelligent, brainy, smart, bright, sharp, proactive, deft, quick-witted, keen, astute, masterful, knowledgeable, proficient, skillful.

respectable
1. deserving honor or respect; worthy, honorable, commendable, admirable, esteemed, reputable, respected, meritorious, virtuous, praiseworthy, reliable, trustworthy, dependable, upright, truthful, honest, principled. **2.** marked by approved standards of conduct; becoming, proper, seemly, well-bred, decorous, decent, modest.

respected
highly regarded or appreciated; revered, esteemed, valued, admired, appreciated, prized, loved, adored, cherished.

respectful
showing or having respect; polite, mannerly, well-bred, decorous, seemly, proper, obeisant, regardful, considerate, thoughtful, attentive, accommodating, cordial, courteous, gracious, deferential.

resplendent
marked by extraordinary elegance, beauty and splendor; magnificent, glorious, superb, gorgeous, sublime, brilliant, radiant, gleaming, dazzling, sparkling, splendid, scintillating, divine, marvelous, wonderful.

responsible
able to be depended upon or trusted; reliable, dependable, trustworthy, solid, steady, sure, accountable, reputable, honorable, creditable, conscientious, moral, ethical, upright, honest, faithful.

responsive
reacting favorably with sympathy, warmth or understanding; amenable, sympathetic, sensitive, kind, good, friendly, receptive, open-minded, approachable, warm, welcoming, broad-minded, fair, just, reasonable.

restful
affording rest; tranquil, peaceful, serene, quiet, quiescent, relaxing.

revered
regarded with great devotion and awe; respected, exalted, esteemed, acclaimed, prestigious, preeminent, venerable, redoubtable, honorable.

reverent
feeling or showing reverence; reverential, respectful, deferential, decorous, proper, devout, religious, godly, pious, spiritual.

rewarding
marked by pleasure or satisfaction; pleasing, satisfying, fulfilling, gratifying.

rich
characterized by great abundance or productivity; prosperous, abundant, wealthy, affluent, fortunate, healthy, flourishing, thriving, successful, fertile, prolific, productive: *Garnett is rich in friendship and talent.*

right
moral, just or good; proper, ethical, righteous, principled, impartial, equitable, right-minded, virtuous, honorable, scrupulous, upright, noble, honest, square, responsible, accountable.

righteous
doing what is right and good; virtuous, scrupulous, upright, irreproachable, honorable, just, honest, reputable, trustworthy, meritorious, commendable.

right-minded
marked by principles of right or good thinking; moral, principled, proper, ethical, virtuous, honest, honorable, scrupulous, square, noble, high-minded.

risible
capable of arousing laughter; funny, humorous, amusing, laughable, droll, comical, farcical, zany, lively, pleasurable, sportive, witty, jocular, jovial: *Linda's risible humor made the party come alive.*

ritzy
very elegant and fashionable; classy, high-class, luxurious, sumptuous, posh, snazzy, chic, stylish, urbane, sophisticated, cosmopolitan.

robust
characterized by strength and vigor; sturdy, sinewy, brawny, hearty, fit, hardy, hale, husky, strong, healthy, vigorous, vital, red-blooded, lively, energetic, sound, powerful, potent, puissant, stalwart, rugged, booming, flourishing, prospering, thriving.

romantic
marked by thoughts or feelings of love and romance; loving, sensitive, tender, compassionate, considerate, ardent, amorous, fervent, emotional, passionate, impassioned, poetic, sentimental.

royal
befitting or resembling a queen or king; regal, dignified, noble, proud, stately, distinguished, honorable, grand, splendid, awesome, superb, magnificent, impressive, first-class, fine, excellent, queenly, kingly, princely: *a royal welcome.*

S

sagacious
possessing keen discernment, sound judgment and farsightedness; wise, sage, sapient, prudent, judicious, sound, rational, commonsensical, shrewd, astute, savvy, canny, acute, sharp, knowing, perspicacious, perceptive, discerning, insightful, smart, intelligent, apt, ingenious, bright, agile, quick, enlightened, versed, aware, farsighted.

sage
possessing or showing great wisdom; wise, sagacious, sapient, commonsensical, logical, sensible, discreet, prudent, judicious.

saintly
like a saint as in reverence or virtue; holy, godly, pious, reverent, devout, religious, faithful, righteous, moral, upright, right-minded, just, good, virtuous, innocent, pure, chaste.

sanguine
expecting a favorable outcome or dwelling on hopeful aspects; upbeat, optimistic, hopeful, confident, positive, assured, cheerful, blithe, light-hearted, sunny, buoyant, carefree, lively, spirited, happy, enthusiastic: *a sanguine outlook.*

sapient
wise or sage; sagacious, reasonable, sensible, commonsensical, prudent, judicious, shrewd, astute, savvy, clever, penetrating, percipient, canny, knowing, insightful, smart, apt, ingenious, bright, agile, quick-witted, knowledgeable, versed, enlightened, aware, farsighted.

satisfying
marked by pleasure or satisfaction; pleasing, rewarding, fulfilling, gratifying.

savvy
well-informed and perceptive; sharp, acute, astute, shrewd, incisive, keen, sensitive, responsive, open, aware, alert, cognizant, insightful, knowing, understanding, sagacious, sapient, wise, discriminating, perspicacious, percipient, smart, quick-witted.

scholarly
marked by profound knowledge and scholarship; scholastic, intellectual, learned, knowledgeable, academic, erudite, intelligent, cultured, versed, literary, studious, well-educated, well-read, well-informed, profound, deep, sage, aware, enlightened.

scrupulous
showing or having a strict regard for what is right; principled, ethical, high-minded, upright, righteous, moral, just, conscionable, honorable, upstanding, good, sincere, earnest, conscientious, prudent, judicious.

secure
having a firm belief in one's own powers; sure, strong, firm, stable, self-confident, self-assured, self-possessed, determined, staunch, certain, positive.

sedate
serenely deliberate and dignified in character or manner; calm, quiet, serene, collected, self-controlled, self-possessed, proper, decorous, refined, genteel.

sedulous
marked by steady attention and effort; industrious, assiduous, diligent, untiring, indefatigable, unfaltering, determined, resolute, persistent, persevering, patient, devoted, conscientious, scrupulous, steady, studious, thorough, focused: *The sedulous contractors worked around the clock to finish the job.*

seemly
1. marked by propriety in behavior or character; right, proper, decent, decorous, nice, respectable, well-behaved, mannerly, judicious, polite, prudent, tactful, diplomatic, genteel, polished, refined. **2.** having a pleasing appearance; attractive, handsome, good-looking, pretty, beautiful, fair, comely, bonny.

select
exceptionally good of its kind; first-rate, great, fine, excellent, superior, first-class, prime, splendid, superb, capital, top, topflight.

selective
showing careful judgment or fine taste; discriminating, discerning, particular, cultivated, cultured, refined.

self-accepting
having acceptance of one's own worth; self-satisfied, self-content, self-assured, happy, positive, sure, confident, secure.

self-actualizing
able to develop or achieve one's full potential; autonomous, independent, self-directed, self-motivated, self-contained, self-reliant.

self-asserting
asserting oneself or one's own rights or views; positive, confident, sure, assured, certain, daring, outspoken.

self-assured
having a firm belief in one's own powers; self-confident, assured, secure, self-possessed, certain, positive, sure, strong, staunch, determined.

self-composed
being or appearing composed; self-possessed, self-contained, cool, calm, self-poised, imperturbable, together, collected, even-tempered, balanced, steady, serene, placid.

self-confident
having a firm belief in one's own powers; self-assured, self-possessed, confident, secure, assured, sure, certain, positive, undoubting, unflinching, unwavering.

self-contained
characterized by self-sufficiency or composure; self-sufficient, self-reliant, self-possessed, self-poised, independent, assured, sure, secure, composed, cool, balanced, poised, imperturbable, even-tempered.

self-content
content with oneself; self-satisfied, glad, pleased, happy, cheerful, relaxed.

self-controlled
having control over one's own emotions or actions; self-possessed, disciplined, moderate, temperate, controlled, calm, cool, balanced, poised, imperturbable.

self-disciplined
having discipline of oneself, one's actions or one's feelings; self-controlled, disciplined, self-directed, self-determined, self-motivated..

self-made
having achieved success or recognition by one's own efforts; self-designed.

self-motivated
able to motivate oneself; motivated, disciplined, self-starting, ambitious, self-directed, industrious, intent, earnest, avid, enthusiastic, energetic, dynamic, zealous, sure, resolute.

self-poised
having a calm, confident manner; self-possessed, self-composed, self-contained, collected, calm, cool, poised, imperturbable, cool-headed, together, sedate, even-tempered, serene, tranquil, balanced, steady.

self-possessed
in control of oneself; self-controlled, self-poised, self-contained, calm, cool, composed, collected, level-headed, balanced, imperturbable, even-tempered, easygoing, tranquil.

self-reliant
relying on one's own abilities or resources; self-sufficient, self-contained, self-supporting, self-assured, self-determined, sure, confident, secure, independent.

self-satisfied
having satisfaction with oneself or one's achievements; self-content, pleased, glad, content, fulfilled, happy, cheerful, sunny, calm, peaceful, carefree, relaxed.

self-starting
capable of undertaking a project on one's own initiative; self-directed, self-determined, self-motivated, self-disciplined, autonomous.

self-sufficient
able to provide for oneself without the help of others; self-supporting, self-determined, independent, self-reliant, confident, assured, secure.

self-trusting
trusting in one's own powers; self-confident, self-assured, secure, sure, positive, undoubting, unwavering.

sensational
arousing strong curiosity, interest or reaction; wonderful, superb, terrific, glorious, splendid, outstanding, spectacular, fantastic, remarkable, fabulous, extraordinary, marvelous, phenomenal, astonishing, amazing, breathtaking, stunning, exciting, stirring, thrilling, compelling.

sensible
marked by good sense or good judgment; rational, reasonable, responsible, sage, sapient, wise, judicious, prudent, level-headed, commonsensical, practical, logical, discriminating, discreet, politic, farsighted, astute, thoughtful, reflective, clearheaded, intelligent.

sensitive
marked by perceptions of great accuracy and sensitivity; perceptive, sharp, acute, keen, intuitive, aware, insightful, delicate, discriminating, discreet, tactful, subtle, sympathetic, compassionate, understanding, kind, concerned, caring, gentle, feeling, warm, responsive, tender-hearted.

sensuous
stimulating or enjoying the pleasure of the senses; sensitive, feeling, responsive, luscious, delicious, luxurious.

sentimental
having or displaying romantic or tender feelings; emotional, romantic, warm, tender, loving, feeling, soft-hearted, sensitive, compassionate.

serene
1. not easily excited or flustered; collected, composed, together, cool, relaxed, carefree, easygoing, casual, laid-back, placid, sedate, poised, balanced, imperturbable, steady, even-tempered, self-possessed, unflappable, unruffled. **2.** tranquil; peaceful, calm, quiet, restful.

serious
marked by depth or sincerity of feeling; earnest, fervent, ardent, passionate, intense, resolute, diligent, intent, firm, determined, devoted, purposeful, committed, sincere, thoughtful, heartfelt.

sharp
1. mentally bright, original and quick; intelligent, smart, brilliant, apt, talented, precocious, alert, acute, keen, shrewd, quick-witted, ready, capable, facile, resourceful, efficient, adept, inventive, creative, ingenious. **2.** fashionable; elegant, chic, stylish, dashing, natty, swank, dapper, snazzy, jaunty, well-dressed, rakish, spruce.

sharp-sighted
marked by keen perception; astute, perceptive, acute, discriminating, alert, sharp, quick, perspicacious, discerning, prudent, watchful, mindful, cautious, vigilant, bright, clear-headed.

sharp-witted
mentally bright, original and quick; clever, intelligent, apt, smart, sharp, precocious, alert, acute, keen, ready, quick-witted, capable, facile, adept, resourceful, creative, inventive, ingenious.

shining
beaming with contentment, joy or love; glowing, bubbling, sparkling, smiling, radiant, bright, aglow, gay, cheery, happy, pleased, delighted, blissful, glad, gleeful, sunny, joyous, animated, light-hearted, convivial, playful, mirthful, elated, frolicsome, enthusiastic, excited.

shrewd
clever or astute in practical matters; sharp, keen, acute, apt, ready, adept, proficient, perspicacious, knowing, discerning, perceptive, wise, sage, sagacious, smart, bright, intelligent, ingenious, creative, resourceful.

significant
having special value or importance; important, meaningful, essential, vital, valuable, big, great, principal, leading, foremost, special, eminent, prominent, notable, noteworthy, outstanding, worthy, meritorious, remarkable, influential, powerful, deep, profound.

simple
free from guile, cunning or deceit; natural, innocent, naive, unaffected, guileless, ingenuous, unpretentious, plain, modest, candid, aboveboard, open, straightforward, square, frank, direct, sincere, honest, decent, fair, equitable, righteous, upright.

sincere
devoid of any hypocrisy or pretense; real, true, honest, genuine, heartfelt, unaffected, good, authentic, earnest, ingenuous, natural, artless, guileless, innocent, naive, simple, pure, open, candid, plain, truthful, veracious, frank, straightforward.

sinewy
having physical strength or power; burly, muscular, sturdy, brawny, robust, husky, strapping, wiry, solid, rugged, athletic, strong, stalwart, doughty, able-bodied, powerful, mighty: *the sinewy runners.*

single-hearted
sincere and dedicated in feeling or spirit; devoted, faithful, committed, loyal, persevering, true.

singular
far beyond what is usual, normal or customary; unique, one-of-a-kind, rare, unusual, distinctive, special, uncommon, exceptional, notable, striking, significant, outstanding, remarkable, wonderful, amazing, impressive, incomparable.

sisterly
characteristic of, or befitting a sister; kind, affectionate, loyal, friendly, kindly, caring, thoughtful, amicable, sociable, affable, congenial, cordial.

skillful
proficient as a result of study and practice; skilled, accomplished, practiced, polished, learned, versed, talented, gifted, proficient, expert, professional, masterful, adept, competent, capable, able, handy, facile, clever, adroit, apt.

slender
gracefully slim; lean, willowy, delicate, svelte, lissome, lithe.

smart
1. intelligent, quick and original; bright, brilliant, knowledgeable, well-read, intellectual, learned, brainy, quick-witted, clever, alert, keen, ready, astute, shrewd, savvy, perceptive, wise, sage, enlightened, insightful, ingenious, resourceful, creative, inventive, competent, apt, adept, facile, able. **2.** attractive and fashionable in style; modish, dapper, chic, stylish, sharp, dashing, jaunty, elegant, classy, natty, spruce, rakish.

smashing
extraordinarily impressive or fine; wonderful, splendid, sensational, glorious, marvelous, astounding, terrific, superb, incredible, amazing, fabulous, prodigious, stupendous, phenomenal.

smooth
marked by facility, especially of expression; elegant, graceful, fluid, effortless, able, skillful, articulate, fluent, suave, urbane, well-bred, cultivated, cultured, polished, refined, trained.

snappy
1. lively and energetic; brisk, alive, active, vigorous, dynamic, sprightly, spry, vivacious, bouncy, animated, spirited, chipper, frisky. **2.** smart in appearance; fashionable, modish, chic, dapper, stylish, dashing, classy, elegant, natty, spruce, sharp, jaunty.

snazzy
smart in appearance or dress; stylish, chic, fashionable, modish, dapper, dashing, elegant, classy, swank, ritzy, natty, spruce, rakish, jaunty.

sociable
enjoying companionship and friendly conversation; social, companionable, congenial, gregarious, convivial, outgoing, neighborly, hospitable, cordial, genial, affable, gracious, amiable, harmonious, kind, couthie, pleasant, good-natured, easygoing, kind-hearted, pleasing.

social
enjoying the company of others; sociable, congenial, companionable, gregarious, convivial, friendly, outgoing, neighborly, hospitable.

soft-hearted
marked by a kind, considerate nature; gentle, tender, loving, compassionate, humane, good, decent, beneficent, benign, good-natured, magnanimous, charitable, generous, affable, amiable, genial, cordial, sympathetic, forbearing, lenient, clement, thoughtful, helpful, understanding, accommodating, gracious, warm, courteous.

solicitous
1. characterized by polite concern for others; thoughtful, courteous, polite, regardful, heedful, attentive, gallant, considerate. **2.** eager to please; earnest, ardent, fervent, fervid, enthusiastic.

solid
capable of being depended upon; responsible, dependable, reliable, trustworthy, level-headed, sensible, constant, steadfast, stalwart, true-blue, loyal, faithful.

soothing
able to soothe or quiet; comforting, calming, consoling, quieting, lulling, gentling: *a soothing touch.*

sophisticated
having worldly knowledge or experience; cosmopolitan, worldly-wise, intellectual, knowledgeable, thoughtful, hip, cool, suave, urbane, elegant, stylish, polished, cultured, educated, realistic, experienced.

sparkling
marked by amusing wit or high spirits; smart, clever, bright, witty, scintillating, ebullient, vivacious, effervescent, exuberant, buoyant, sprightly, animated, enthusiastic, zesty, energetic, lively.

special
distinct among others of a kind; unique, distinctive, singular, novel, unusual, uncommon, unequaled, peerless, inimitable, incomparable, important, notable, memorable, outstanding, exceptional, rare, extraordinary, remarkable.

spectacular
overwhelmingly impressive; stunning, sensational, striking, grand, breathtaking, magnificent, extraordinary, smashing, brilliant, remarkable, phenomenal, gorgeous, superb, splendid, glorious, divine, terrific, exceptional, marvelous, wonderful, fantastic.

speedy
characterized by great swiftness; quick, fast, swift, fleet, celeritous, snappy, prompt, expeditious.

spellbinding
to captivate with or as if with magic; enchanting, charming, bewitching, entrancing, enthralling, captivating, fascinating, mesmerizing, amazing, compelling, enrapturing, riveting.

spiffy
smart in appearance or dress; stylish, dapper, neat, natty, snazzy, snappy, spruce, sharp, rakish, gay, jaunty, swank, well-dressed, ritzy.

spirited
characterized by a lively, eager quality; vibrant, dynamic, sparkling, alive, buoyant, energetic, vivacious, bright, chipper, enthusiastic, excited, animated, ebullient, ardent, avid, spunky, brave, valiant, courageous, heroic, game, feisty, high-spirited.

spiritual
marked by concern with the human soul; godly, religious, worshipful, humble, devout, devoted, pious, reverent, moral, righteous, virtuous.

splendid
1. marked by great admiration; notable, admirable, illustrious, distinguished, eminent, renowned, famous, celebrated, honorable, exalted, venerable, laudable, noble, prominent, memorable, peerless, meritorious. **2.** marked by particular excellence; wonderful, glorious, superb, marvelous, sensational, terrific, outstanding, supreme, exceptional, regal, grand, stately, striking, gorgeous, august, elegant, graceful, dazzling, magnificent, majestic, excellent, extraordinary, smashing, fantastic, stupendous.

spontaneous
arising from a natural impulse or desire; instinctive, instinctual, free, natural, intuitive, unrehearsed.

sporting
characterized by sportsmanship; fair, clean, sportsmanlike, square, just.

sportive
full of fun, high spirits and humor; high-spirited, frolicsome, playful, fun-loving, mischievous, impish, devilish, elfish, waggish, coltish, frisky, humorous, amusing, funny, witty, jocund, jocular.

sprightly
full of spirit and vitality; active, lively, frisky, brisk, dynamic, light, energetic, carefree, blithe, debonair, peppy, spry, nimble, agile, yare, animated, spirited, vivacious, jaunty, breezy, buoyant, gay, sparkling, snappy, chipper, enthusiastic, hearty, playful, sportive, joyful.

spry
moving or thinking quickly and easily; active, alive, deft, lively, brisk, facile, nimble, agile, lithe, well-coordinated, supple, alert, keen, quick-witted, sharp, bright, smart, acute.

spunky
being spirited, courageous and determined; vibrant, high-spirited, lively, alive, dynamic, sparkling, bright, chipper, energetic, vivacious, fervent, ardent, eager, keen, intense, enthusiastic, daring, brave, valiant, heroic, game, plucky, mettlesome, gutsy, stout, resolute.

stable
consistently reliable; steady, sure, responsible, dependable, sensible, trustworthy, level-headed, true-blue, constant, steadfast, staunch, faithful, resolute, determined, persevering.

stalwart
characterized by bravery or strong determination; courageous, brave, bold, heroic, fearless, chivalrous, gallant, dashing, adventurous, stout, daring, gutsy, intrepid, mettlesome, valorous, audacious, doughty, game, resolute, unwavering, indefatigable, determined, steadfast, persistent, devoted, faithful, true, constant, steady, purposeful, dauntless, plucky, spunky, red-blooded.

stately
characterized by dignity and grace; august, dignified, distinguished, regal, queenly, princely, kingly, royal, noble, grand, magnificent, splendid, resplendent, marvelous, superb, majestic, sublime, elevated, awesome, imposing, striking.

statuesque
like a statue in dignity or grace; stately, imposing, dignified, regal, majestic, splendid, noble, grand, graceful, elegant.

staunch
marked by strong determination; steadfast, indefatigable, unwavering, resolute, determined, persevering, dauntless, firm, devoted, dedicated, true, fast, constant, purposeful, steady, plucky, game, mettlesome, spunky, red-blooded.

steadfast
constant in purpose or resolution; firm, staunch, resolute, determined, persevering, true, steady, devoted, dedicated, unswerving.

steady
capable of being depended upon; reliable, dependable, responsible, conscientious, firm, faithful, true, solid, steadfast, devoted, constant.

sterling
exceptionally good; extraordinary, exquisite, precious, remarkable, priceless, matchless, splendid, outstanding, superlative, excellent, fine, prime, choice, first-class, superb, worthy, admirable, notable, estimable: *a sterling reputation.*

stimulating
inspiring greater action or effort; enlivening, vitalizing, motivating, encouraging, uplifting, cheering: *a stimulating discussion.*

stirring
affecting or inspiring deep emotions; impressive, poignant, effective, tender, moving, touching, exciting, breathtaking, thrilling, soul-stirring.

stout-hearted
characterized by courage and valor; courageous, bold, heroic, fearless, gallant, chivalrous, brave, dashing, adventurous, daring, lionhearted, stout, gutsy, valorous, audacious, intrepid, doughty, game, staunch, steadfast, resolute, stalwart, plucky, mettlesome, undaunted, unfaltering.

straight
speaking or spoken sincerely and freely; straightforward, open, direct, honest, candid, undisguised, plain, free, outspoken, frank, uninhibited, genuine, guileless, square, sincere, ingenuous, aboveboard.

straightforward
marked by honesty and frankness; straight, honest, direct, open, free-spoken, forthright, frank, explicit.

strapping
physically healthy and strong; husky, robust, able-bodied, athletic, burly, hale, hearty, rugged, solid, sound, stalwart, sturdy, vigorous, powerful.

striking
having a strong impression on the senses or mind; arresting, imposing, outstanding, eye-catching, grand, august, impressive, unforgettable, memorable, majestic, awesome, marvelous, stupendous, astounding, incredible, fabulous, exceptional, wonderful, unique, superb, great, magnificent, brilliant, dazzling, stunning, beautiful, gorgeous, handsome, good-looking.

strong
1. marked by great physical strength or good health; powerful, husky, burly, well-built, muscular, puissant, mighty, hardy, athletic, red-blooded, active, hearty, strapping, brawny, sturdy, healthy, whole, sound, well, fit, wholesome, energetic, vigorous, robust, spirited. **2.** morally powerful or courageous; stalwart, resolute, intrepid, steadfast, indefatigable, unwavering, loyal, dedicated, moral, ethical, stout-hearted, brave, heroic, valiant, mettlesome.

strong-willed
having a powerful will; determined, resolute, persevering, persistent, indefatigable, dauntless, purposeful, staunch, steadfast, dedicated, true, devoted, loyal, constant, steady, firm, stable, earnest, confident, serious, self-possessed.

studious
1. marked by steady attention and effort; industrious, diligent, steady, assiduous, sedulous, thorough, earnest, intense, tireless, untiring, persevering, unfaltering. **2.** marked by a fondness for learning; scholarly, intellectual, academic, erudite, cultured, lettered.

stunning
1. extremely attractive or good-looking; glorious, magnificent, divine, superb, exquisite, gorgeous, ravishing, beautiful, lovely, fetching. **2.** surprisingly spectacular; sublime, astonishing, splendid, impressive, amazing, extraordinary, incredible, marvelous, wondrous, fabulous, sensational, dazzling, resplendent, brilliant.

sturdy
physically strong and healthy; strapping, able-bodied, vigorous, robust, solid, stalwart, muscular, sinewy, brawny, burly, rugged, husky, mighty, puissant, powerful, athletic, hardy, hale.

stylish
attractive and fashionable in style; smart, chic, modish, dapper, sharp, elegant, natty, classy, jaunty, well-dressed, dashing, spruce, rakish.

suave
having a smooth and courteous manner; urbane, worldly, polite, sophisticated, pleasant, agreeable, tactful, diplomatic.

substantial
having considerable importance; important, consequential, influential, prestigious, powerful, meaningful, vital, essential, principal, leading, outstanding, foremost, prominent, great, noteworthy, remarkable: *a substantial contribution to science.*

subtle
capable of understanding or making fine distinctions; astute, shrewd, sagacious, discerning, sensitive, aware, cognizant, percipient, clever, ingenious, expert, apt, proficient, experienced, versed, sophisticated.

successful
achieving, having or resulting in success; flourishing, booming, thriving, fortunate, prosperous, wealthy, affluent, rich, triumphant, victorious, impressive, important, famous, renowned.

sunny
being in or showing good spirits; happy, bright, cheery, optimistic, merry, gay, blithe, carefree, happy-go-lucky, bubbly, alive, smiling, aglow, glowing, pleasing, joyous, jocund, mirthful, festive, amiable, convivial, lively, chipper, fresh, dynamic, vivacious, animated, spirited, sprightly, jaunty, playful, sparkling, blissful.

superb
exceptionally good of its kind; great, excellent, superior, prime, first-rate, fine, capital, champion, topflight, magnificent, splendid, superlative, striking, matchless, exemplary, remarkable, extraordinary, notable, eminent, sensational, incredible, resplendent, brilliant, dazzling, amazing, stunning, terrific, fantastic.

superior
greater or higher in quality or degree of it's kind; extraordinary, remarkable, smashing, marvelous, wonderful, super, exceptional, excellent, notable, estimable, topnotch, superlative, striking, matchless, nonpareil, perfect, sterling, first-rate, choice.

superlative
of the highest degree or quality; superb, paramount, supreme, super, preeminent, foremost, best, capital, prime, first-rate, excellent, topnotch, unexcelled, incomparable, unique, inimitable, matchless, nonpareil, singular, sublime, extraordinary, exceptional, remarkable, fantastic, dazzling, wonderful, splendid.

supportive
affording encouragement, support or aid; helpful, understanding, kind, encouraging, sympathetic, loving, humane, benevolent, beneficent, benignant, altruistic, considerate, compassionate, thoughtful, gentle, tender, lenient, kind-hearted, amicable, cordial, gracious.

supreme
greatest in importance, quality or degree; paramount, preeminent, foremost, best, leading, crowning, prime, superlative, incomparable, unexcelled, excellent, inimitable, unequaled, nonpareil, sublime, consummate, extraordinary.

sure
characterized by assurance or strong belief; secure, assured, confident, steady, self-assured, self-possessed, certain, positive, undoubting.

sure-footed
unlikely to stumble or falter; agile, spry, graceful, brisk, speedy, quick, light, fleet, nimble-footed: *the sure-footed hiker.*

svelte
slender and graceful; lithe, limber, lithesome, lissome, willowy, fine, delicate, elegant.

sweet
possessing a pleasing disposition; lovable, pleasant, amiable, gracious, likable, good-natured, congenial, couthie, polite, cordial, courteous, friendly, sociable, accommodating, winsome, charming, appealing, engaging, fetching, bewitching, entrancing, prepossessing.

sympathetic
comprehending the needs, feelings and views of others; understanding, empathic, compassionate, caring, concerned, comforting, supportive, loving, generous, big, big-hearted, humane, kind, kindly, good-natured, warm, charitable, gentle, tender, considerate, thoughtful, patient, agreeable, brotherly, sisterly.

systematic
characterized by an orderly method; organized, well-organized, steady, methodical, well-planned, well-prepared, efficient, effective, effectual, businesslike, thorough.

T

tactful
having or showing sensitivity and skill in dealing with others; discreet, prudent, discriminating, discerning, diplomatic, politic, judicious, wise, sage, sagacious, sapient, mindful, considerate, sensitive, circumspect, perspicacious, keen, perceptive, skillful, shrewd, urbane, suave, mannerly, polished, gracious.

talented
characterized by a natural aptitude or ability; gifted, endowed, clever, artistic, smart, ingenious, intelligent, bright, deft, apt, adept, dexterous, able, capable, competent, proficient, expert, skillful, masterful, polished, first-rate, topnotch.

tasteful
marked by a good sense of what is beautiful, excellent or appropriate; artistic, aesthetic, elegant, charming, graceful, cultured, finished, refined, sensitive, aware, discriminating, tactful, polite, proper, decorous.

teachable
marked by a capacity for or interest in learning; able, smart, bright, keen, quick, sharp, inquisitive, curious, conscientious, scholarly, studious, diligent, industrious, trainable, open-minded, amenable, agreeable, eager, enthusiastic.

telegenic
characterized by qualities or a physical appearance that televise well; videogenic.

temperate
marked by moderate or self-restrained behavior; reasonable, conservative, discreet, composed, collected, cool-headed, poised, level-headed, balanced, rational, sensible, peaceful, unruffled, quiet, self-disciplined, self-possessed.

tender
1. possessing a kindly, considerate nature; gentle, mild, considerate, solicitous, soft-hearted, protective, compassionate. **2.** showing warmth of feeling; loving, adoring, devoted, affectionate, romantic.

tender-hearted
easily moved by the distress of another; compassionate, sensitive, sympathetic, concerned, thoughtful, understanding, supportive, caring, comforting, magnanimous, humane, generous, good-natured, helpful, kind, warm, neighborly, friendly, merciful, charitable, big-hearted, giving, benevolent, benignant.

terrific
particularly excellent; wonderful, splendid, glorious, marvelous, super, sensational, awesome, exceptional, outstanding, smashing, superior, great, fine, first-class, sterling, admirable, notable, remarkable.

thankful
feeling or showing gratitude; grateful, appreciative, pleased.

thorough
marked by attentiveness to details; careful, precise, accurate, particular, conscientious, detailed, meticulous, scrupulous, methodical.

thoroughbred
characterized by good breeding and education; elegant, graceful, gentle, genteel, refined, polished, cultured, well-bred, well-mannered, polite, courteous, courtly, gracious, classy, ladylike, gentlemanly, sophisticated, urbane, worldly, cosmopolitan.

thoughtful
1. marked by polite concern for the well-being of others; considerate, courteous, polite, solicitous, patient, compassionate, sympathetic, tender, kindly, respectful, benefic, deferent, regardful, benevolent, charitable. **2.** characterized by careful thought; circumspect, prudent, discreet, attentive, watchful, heedful, careful: *a thoughtful question.*

thrifty
prudent in the use of resources; frugal, economical, canny, provident, careful, temperate, moderate, conservative.

thrilling
able to produce great pleasure; stirring, exciting, inspiring, arousing, stimulating, moving, electrifying, rousing, captivating, exhilarating.

tidy
in good order or clean condition; neat, trim, spruce, orderly, well-ordered, well-organized, clean.

tireless
having a capacity for protracted effort; indefatigable, inexhaustible, unflagging, untiring, courageous, rugged, stalwart, intrepid, resolute, staunch, dogged, determined, firm, steadfast, indomitable, enduring, hardy, unwavering.

tolerant
marked by acceptance or respect for the behaviors, beliefs or opinions of others; liberal, progressive, open, broad-minded, enlightened, kind, amenable, reasonable, fair, just, unbiased, impartial, understanding, good-natured, charitable, lenient, clement, forbearing.

topflight
of the foremost rank or highest quality; topnotch, excellent, fine, first-rate, superior, superlative, superb, capital, best, exceptional, outstanding, crowning, greatest, matchless, unsurpassed.

topnotch
exceptionally good of its kind; fine, topflight, excellent, superior, great, superb, splendid, prime, first-rate, select, champion.

touching
affecting or stirring the emotions; impressive, poignant, tender, soul-stirring, moving, striking, exciting, thrilling, breathtaking.

trainable
having a capacity for or interest in learning; teachable, amenable, open, ready, smart, able, bright, quick, alert, sharp, studious, industrious, diligent, conscientious, inquisitive.

tranquil
1. not easily excited or flustered; collected, composed, together, cool, relaxed, imperturbable, unruffled, self-possessed, carefree, laid-back, steady, easygoing, casual, placid, poised, balanced. **2.** serene; calm, peaceful, quiet, restful.

treasured
highly regarded; cherished, revered, esteemed, loved, adored, valued, appreciated, respected, prized.

tremendous
arousing admiration or wonder; superb, splendid, glorious, terrific, sensational, incredible, amazing, fabulous, super, great, astounding, miraculous, stupendous, marvelous, phenomenal, wondrous, remarkable, extraordinary, breathtaking, divine, stunning, exceptional, smashing, excellent, first-class, superior.

tried and true
tested and proved to be worthy or good; dependable, reliable, steady, responsible, trusty, trustworthy, honest, honorable, sure, reputable.

true
characterized by faithfulness or truthfulness; loyal, constant, firm, steady, faithful, resolute, steadfast, devoted, true-blue, dutiful, reliable, dependable, trustworthy, earnest, sincere, honest, incorruptible, scrupulous, veracious, straight.

true-blue
faithful as to a person, cause or duty; loyal, constant, fast, faithful, resolute, staunch, dedicated, dutiful, yeomanly, stable, solid, reliable, steady, trustworthy.

trusting
full of trust; trustful, confident, sure, certain, positive, definite, secure.

trustworthy
capable of being trusted or relied upon; dependable, responsible, reliable, tried and true, honorable, incorruptible, reputable, credible, believable, straight, honest, genuine, sincere, ingenuous, aboveboard, true-blue, loyal, faithful, steadfast, constant, unwavering, dedicated.

truthful
characterized by honesty and openness; honest, true, honorable, incorruptible, veracious, righteous, upright, upstanding, decent, moral, principled, ethical, virtuous, open, direct, straight, frank, forthright, candid, straightforward, genuine, real, sincere, unaffected, heartfelt.

U

ultramodern
extremely modern in ideas or style; progressive, advanced, avant-garde, modernistic, forward-looking.

unaffected
free from affectation or pretension; sincere, genuine, real, natural, naive, artless, innocent, simple, guileless, true, ingenuous, honest, forthright, frank, candid, straight, direct, down-to-earth, unpretentious, unstudied.

unafraid
possessing or showing courage; fearless, bold, heroic, courageous, brave, dashing, gallant, chivalrous, adventurous, daring, mettlesome, dauntless, intrepid, valiant, gutsy, audacious, doughty, game, plucky, steadfast, resolved, lionhearted, stout-hearted, unwavering.

unambiguous
expressing or expressed clearly and fully; positive, definite, decisive, precise, clear, explicit, accurate, distinct, plain.

unassuming
modest in manner or nature; humble, unpretentious, unaffected, natural, ingenuous, down-to-earth.

unbiased
free of bias or judgment; impartial, fair, liberal, objective, square, just, equitable, nonpartisan, neutral, nonjudgmental, unprejudiced, judicious, open-minded.

unblemished
without flaw or blemish; chaste, pure, clean, unstained, unsullied, untarnished: *an unblemished reputation.*

uncommon
far beyond what is usual, normal or customary; unusual, one-of-a-kind, unique, singular, novel, special, rare, distinctive, incomparable, matchless, inimitable, exceptional, remarkable.

unconventional
not conforming to convention; unusual, novel, uncommon, unique, unorthodox, original, individual, singular, distinctive, different: *an unconventional teacher.*

undaunted
resolutely courageous; fearless, bold, brave, heroic, gallant, stout, courageous, unafraid, dauntless, valorous, daring, adventuresome, mettlesome, intrepid, stalwart, persevering, high-spirited, unflagging, indefatigable.

understanding
comprehending the needs, feelings and views of others; compassionate, kindly, sympathetic, empathetic, supportive, generous, big-hearted, good-natured, humane, charitable, tender, gentle, considerate, patient, thoughtful, accepting, forbearing, clement, lenient.

understated
exhibiting restrained good taste; artistic, elegant, graceful, aesthetic, cultured, polished, finished, refined, cultivated, sensitive, discriminating.

unequaled
without equal or rival; matchless, peerless, incomparable, unrivaled, inimitable, nonpareil, consummate, unique, perfect, first-class, sterling, supreme, champion, topnotch, prime, choice, paramount.

unfaltering
having a capacity for protracted effort; indefatigable, inexhaustible, unflagging, rugged, hardy, stalwart, intrepid, resolute, determined, firm, steadfast, persevering, sedulous, indomitable, enduring, unwavering.

unflagging
marked by untiring effort; unfailing, unswerving, unflinching, tireless, unfaltering, indefatigable, rugged, game, hardy, earnest, spunky, intrepid, purposeful, persistent, assiduous.

unflappable
not easily upset or excited; calm, poised, steady, peaceful, collected, cool, undisturbed, imperturbable, self-possessed, unruffled, together, even-tempered, unflustered.

unforgettable
not to be forgotten; memorable, great, illustrious, extraordinary, remarkable, significant, unique, outstanding, special, rare, fantastic, marvelous, powerful, dramatic, eloquent, sensational, thrilling, electrifying, moving, inspiring.

uninhibited
having few inhibitions; easygoing, free, casual, informal, relaxed, natural, earthy, down-to-earth, carefree, artless, open, ingenuous, direct, candid, frank, sincere.

unique
far beyond what is usual, normal or customary; singular, one-of-a-kind, rare, original, distinctive, special, uncommon, exceptional, notable, striking, significant, outstanding, remarkable, wonderful, amazing, impressive, incomparable.

unparalleled
being unsurpassed; unexcelled, nonpareil, matchless, unequaled, incomparable, inimitable, singular, foremost, greatest.

unprejudiced
free of bias or judgment; impartial, fair, liberal, objective, square, just, equitable, nonpartisan, neutral, judicious, unbiased, even-handed, reasonable, broad-minded.

unpretentious
lacking pretension or affectation; simple, modest, unaffected, humble, unassuming, natural, genuine, plain, direct, candid, ingenuous, open, straightforward, honest.

unrivaled
having no rival or equal; unequaled, unparalleled, unsurpassed, peerless, distinctive, unique, topnotch, best, special, superior, champion.

unruffled
not easily flustered or excited; collected, calm, imperturbable, cool-headed, unflappable, even-tempered, self-possessed, unflustered, pacific, together, composed, serene.

unselfish
willing to share freely; generous, magnanimous, munificent, benefic, charitable, benevolent, altruistic, benign, giving, humane, helpful, compassionate, good, considerate, sympathetic, bountiful, big-hearted, kind, good-natured.

unsurpassed
without equal or rival; unparalleled, peerless, unmatchable, unexcelled, nonpareil, unrivaled, incomparable, paramount, preeminent, leading, best, superlative, foremost.

untiring
marked by tireless effort; intrepid, indefatigable, unflagging, hardy, rugged, stalwart, staunch, steadfast, assiduous, sedulous, indomitable, enduring, unflinching.

upbeat
looking on the bright side of things; optimistic, hopeful, sanguine, blithe, positive, confident, light-hearted, cheery, sunny, buoyant, carefree.

uplifting
elevating the spirit; energizing, inspiring, cheering, exhilarating, stimulating, invigorating, exciting, revitalizing, stirring.

uproarious
extremely funny; sidesplitting, hysterical, hilarious, humorous, comical, laughable, sportive, risible, zany, witty, jocose, jesting, jolly, farcical.

upstanding
worthy of honor or respect in principle or action; respectable, reputable, estimable, creditable, honorable, honest, incorruptible, upright, principled, right-minded, moral, proper, virtuous, decent.

urbane
refined and courteous; cultivated, well-bred, civilized, cultured, enlightened, decorous, mannerly, gracious, debonair, cosmopolitan, suave, worldly: *an urbane manner.*

V

valiant
showing or having courage; bold, valorous, adventuresome, fearless, gallant, courageous, chivalrous, daring, dashing, dauntless, stout, brave, gutsy, intrepid, mettlesome, heroic, audacious, game, steadfast, womanly, manly, lionhearted, undismayed, unswerving.

validating
expressing affirmation for; affirming, accepting, esteeming.

valuable
of great value or importance; rare, precious, priceless, choice, fine, excellent, extraordinary, vital, exceptional, important, special, commendable, admirable.

valued
highly respected; revered, loved, adored, beloved, cherished, esteemed, respected, admired, appreciated, prized, treasured.

venerable
commanding great respect by virtue of age or dignity; distinguished, eminent, celebrated, prominent, notable, illustrious, renowned, preeminent, noble, estimable, honorable, revered, respected.

venturesome
willing to take risks; venturous, daring, audacious, adventuresome, enterprising, courageous, brave, bold, gallant, heroic, chivalrous, valorous, intrepid, plucky, spunky, spirited, dauntless, fearless.

veracious
consistently truthful and honest; upright, true, honorable, upstanding, righteous, incorruptible, straight, forthright, candid, plain-spoken, frank, undisguised, genuine, sincere, heartfelt, unfeigned, decent, moral, principled, ethical, virtuous.

vernal
fresh or youthful; fresh, young, active, enthusiastic, optimistic, hopeful, confident, cheerful, light-hearted: *a vernal spirit.*

versatile
having many talents or abilities; talented, multitalented, diversified, eclectic, multifaceted, adaptable, able, handy, clever, resourceful, ingenious.

versed
characterized by knowledge or experience; knowledgeable, learned, scholarly, sage, scholastic, literary, lettered, well-read, well-educated, academic, erudite, sophisticated, savvy, conversant, enlightened, accomplished, masterful, expert.

vibrant
full of life, enthusiasm and energy; lively, alive, spirited, brisk, active, sparkling, glowing, enthusiastic, excited, eager, keen, animated, vivacious, dynamic, vigorous, energetic, chipper.

videogenic
marked by a physical appearance or qualities that televise well; telegenic.

vigilant
keenly attentive; alert, observant, watchful, wide-awake, open-eyed, aware, prepared, mindful, heedful, cautious, prudent, discreet, careful, circumspect.

vigorous
having or showing vigor; energetic, lively, active, dynamic, brisk, spry, vivacious, sparkling, peppy, robust, hardy, hale, strong, healthy, vital, stalwart, staunch, spunky, eager, enthusiastic, ardent, fervent, intense, powerful: *a vigorous personality.*

virile
characteristic of, or befitting the male sex; masculine, manly, strong, powerful, robust, vigorous, hardy, sturdy, athletic, muscular, husky, strapping, hale, hearty, energetic, dynamic, brave, courageous, bold, heroic, valorous, gallant, daring, intrepid, fearless, dauntless, spunky, doughty, mettlesome, spirited.

virtuous
having or showing virtue, especially moral excellence; moral, proper, decent, modest, right, pure, chaste, decorous, nice, becoming, seemly, respectable, dependable, honest, honorable, upright, trustworthy.

vital
1. full of vigor and life; energetic, lively, vivacious, animated, spirited, dynamic, enthusiastic, eager, zestful, vigorous: *a vital spirit.* **2.** of special importance; valuable, essential.

vitalizing
able to stimulate to physical or emotional activity; invigorating, stimulating, energizing, refreshing, enlivening, motivating, uplifting, inspiring.

vivacious
full of joyful, unrestrained high spirits; spirited, exuberant, ebullient, sparkling, brisk, chipper, jaunty, sprightly, buoyant, breezy, merry, cheerful, jovial, mirthful, bright, blithe, light-hearted, frolicsome, playful, bouncy, vibrant, energetic, lively, spunky, active, dynamic, animated, fervent, eager, keen, enthusiastic, excited, zealous.

vivid
1. clear and distinct; colorful, bright, striking, dynamic, impressive. **2.** full of life and energy; animated, alive, vibrant, energetic, vivacious, bouncy, sprightly, spirited, dashing, breezy, gay, peppy, chipper, effervescent.

vocal
frank or open in speech; candid, free, outspoken, straightforward, forthright, direct, unambiguous, explicit, undisguised, uninhibited.

waggish
full of merriment and mischief; mischievous, playful, impish, elfish, fun-loving, devilish, sportive, funny, amusing, witty, clever, jocular, droll, jolly, comical, entertaining, silly, humorous.

warm
marked by kindness or enthusiasm; friendly, cordial, genial, hospitable, amiable, approachable, welcoming, receptive, affectionate, gentle, kind, earnest, sincere, heartfelt, glowing, enthusiastic, lively, animated, energetic, vivacious.

warm-hearted
showing sympathy, kindness or affection; loving, compassionate, sympathetic, kindly, beneficent, benignant, good-natured, generous, magnanimous, altruistic, gracious, helpful, obliging, amiable, affable, nice, cordial, genial, forgiving, lenient, understanding, thoughtful, considerate, courteous, gentle, tender, affectionate, motherly, fatherly, sisterly, brotherly.

watchful
marked by alertness or vigilance; alert, observant, vigilant, attentive, wide-awake, heedful, mindful, aware, circumspect, prudent.

wealthy
marked by abundance, good fortune or success; prosperous, abundant, rich, affluent, fortunate, successful.

welcoming
easily approached; congenial, warm, friendly, easy, genial, affable, open, pleasant, sociable, courteous, polite, gracious, responsive, approachable.

well
1. having good health; healthy, hale, hearty, sound, hardy, sturdy, whole, solid, able-bodied, vigorous, robust, strong, energetic, spirited, rugged, strapping, stalwart. **2.** marked by good fortune; fortunate, prosperous, booming, flourishing, thriving.

well-adjusted
marked by good judgment or composure; reasonable, rational, sensible, prudent, judicious, sapient, sagacious, commonsensical, level-headed, together, well-balanced, self-possessed, undismayed, steady, imperturbable, easygoing, relaxed.

well-balanced
sensible or sane; reasonable, rational, judicious, circumspect, sage, moderate, commonsensical, practical, intelligent, discerning, down-to-earth, well-adjusted, self-possessed, unruffled, cool-headed.

well-bred
characterized by good manners or training; courteous, well-mannered, gracious, polite, charming, elegant, cultured, genteel, refined, polished, ladylike, gentlemanly, sophisticated, urbane, suave.

well-coordinated
moving quickly and easily; agile, active, alive, deft, lively, brisk, facile, nimble, yare, spry, lithe, quick, supple.

well-developed
1. showing or having good physical form; muscular, sturdy, brawny, sinewy, burly, strong, strapping, solid, rugged, wiry, husky, well-built, able-bodied, athletic. **2.** done or thought out in a thorough way; organized, well-prepared, orderly, systematic, detailed, thorough.

well-disposed
marked by kindness, friendliness or sympathy; good, gentle, kindly, tender, compassionate, affectionate, loving, benevolent, benign, humane, decent, magnanimous, generous, altruistic, big-hearted, helpful, obliging, affable, cordial, amiable, friendly, forbearing, sympathetic, lenient, thoughtful, considerate.

well-dressed
carefully groomed and dressed; smart, sleek, natty, nifty, sharp, dapper, chic, fashionable, stylish, dashing, elegant.

well-established
marked by security and reliability; stable, steady, sound, responsible, reliable, dependable, trustworthy.

well-favored
possessing qualities that delight the eye; attractive, handsome, beautiful, fair, lovely, pretty, seemly, comely, bonny, gorgeous, pulchritudinous, ravishing, pleasing, appealing, radiant, wholesome, glowing, graceful, elegant, delicate.

well-founded
based on good judgment or sound reasoning; reasonable, rational, sound, clearheaded, wise, sapient, sensible, prudent, judicious, logical, commonsensical, well-grounded.

well-groomed
carefully groomed and dressed; smart, sleek, natty, dapper, spruce, spiffy, chic, clean-cut, well-dressed.

well-grounded
having or showing sound reasoning; reasonable, sound, rational, sensible, discerning, judicious, level-headed, wise, sagacious, commonsensical, practical, intelligent, thoughtful, well-founded.

well-informed
having much information or knowledge; knowledgeable, literate, literary, learned, educated, erudite, well-read, enlightened, academic, scholarly, conversant, well-versed, intellectual, intelligent, brilliant.

well-intentioned
intending to be helpful; humane, good-natured, big, loving, kindly, supportive, well-meaning, benefic, benevolent, beneficent, altruistic, compassionate, considerate, gentle, unselfish, thoughtful, amicable.

well-known
widely known and esteemed; prominent, notable, illustrious, eminent, famous, distinguished, renowned, celebrated, preeminent, prestigious, legendary, redoubtable, great, acclaimed.

well-mannered
showing or having good manners and consideration for others; polite, respectful, deferential, decorous, proper, tactful, diplomatic, refined, polished, courtly, gallant, courteous, gracious, genteel, mannerly, well-behaved, urbane, cordial, sociable, winning, charming.

well-meaning
meaning to be helpful; humane, good-natured, big, loving, benign, supportive, benevolent, considerate, kind, thoughtful, well-intentioned.

well-prepared
performing or prepared effectively with efficiency and order; organized, orderly, systematic, thorough, well-developed, effective, detailed.

well-read
knowledgeable through having read many books; informed, enlightened, well-educated, scholarly, erudite, academic, lettered, well-versed, cultivated, refined, sophisticated.

well-rounded
having knowledge or information in a wide variety of subjects; well-read, knowledgeable, well-versed, well-informed, enlightened, conversant.

well-spoken
having educated and refined speech; eloquent, fluent, facile, expressive, articulate, graceful, communicative.

well-thought-of
regarded with much respect; esteemed, respected, admired, revered, honored, valued.

well-versed
characterized by knowledge and understanding; intelligent, brilliant, scholarly, learned, versed, literary, well-read, well-educated, academic, intellectual, erudite, cognizant, insightful, cultured, worldly.

whimsical
displaying fancy or whimsy; fanciful, imaginative, creative, romantic, quaint, mischievous, playful, funny.

whole
1. marked by good health; hardy, sound, well, healthy, hearty, hale, wholesome, robust, strong. **2.** complete; fulfilled.

wholehearted
completely sincere or enthusiastic; real, genuine, heartfelt, unreserved, dedicated, fervent, earnest, resolute, single-hearted, eager, high-spirited, energetic.

wholesome
marked by physical, mental or moral soundness; healthy, whole, sound, well, fit, hearty, hale, robust, strong, vigorous, invigorating, refreshing, stimulating: *a wholesome child, a wholesome activity.*

willing
amiable and pleasant in nature; ready, agreeable, accommodating, amiable, congenial, cordial, couthie, gracious, courteous, gentle, friendly, amicable, kind, pleasing, easygoing, good-natured.

willowy
tall, slender and graceful like a willow; limber, lithe, lithesome, lissome, flexible, supple, nimble, agile, svelte, slim, lean.

winning
pleasing to the eye or mind; pretty, lovely, handsome, beautiful, sweet, fair, attractive, winsome, magnetic, appealing, charming, enchanting, fetching, engaging, prepossessing, captivating, enticing, bewitching.

wiry
being strong and lean; sinewy, trim, powerful, muscular, able-bodied, well-built, athletic.

wise
marked by keen discernment, sound judgment or knowledge; sagacious, sage, sapient, astute, aware, shrewd, cognizant, perspicacious, percipient, insightful, discerning, reasonable, sensible, prudent, judicious, well-grounded, conversant, enlightened, bright, scholarly, learned, erudite.

witty
amusing or pleasing because of wit or originality; clever, scintillating, sparkling, humorous, funny, jocular, original, smart, sharp, quick, bright, droll, mirthful, jolly, comic, farcical.

womanly
characteristic of, or befitting the female sex; feminine, ladylike, refined, genteel, gentle, delicate, soft, tender, protective, caring, sympathetic, loving, nurturing, warm, kind, devoted, tireless, enduring, persevering, honorable, courageous, venturesome, strong, spunky, game, spirited, indomitable.

wonderful
stimulating admiration or wonder; wondrous, marvelous, splendid, glorious, sensational, incredible, amazing, super, fantastic, fabulous, astonishing, astounding, terrific, superb, stupendous, phenomenal, extraordinary, remarkable, divine, breathtaking, smashing, excellent, great, first-class, superior.

worldly
having worldly knowledge or experience; sophisticated, urbane, cosmopolitan, worldly-wise, hip, polished, cultivated, cultured, realistic, practical, experienced.

worldly-wise
wise in the ways of the world; urbane, sophisticated, cosmopolitan, hip, cool, knowing, experienced.

worshipful
feeling or showing reverence; reverent, adoring, devout, pious, respectful, faithful, prayerful.

worthy
deserving admiration, honor or respect; admirable, commendable, meritorious, praiseworthy, laudable, respectable, estimable, valuable, honorable, reputable, exemplary, excellent, noble, decent, righteous, honest, virtuous.

X

***ex*cellent**
exceptionally good; great, fine, superior, prime, choice, splendid, superb, capital, exceptional, first-class, champion, outstanding, first-rate, superlative, remarkable.

***ex*ceptional**
far above average; outstanding, magnificent, preeminent, unique, rare, remarkable, extraordinary, phenomenal, singular, superior, excellent.

***ex*citing**
able to produce excitement; stirring, moving, inspiring, stimulating, thrilling, motivating, electrifying, captivating, exhilarating.

***ex*emplary**
deserving of imitation; admirable, commendable, meritorious, notable, laudable, praiseworthy, noteworthy, model, perfect, ideal, consummate, outstanding, superb, superior, excellent.

***ex*hilarating**
enlivening or making cheerful; invigorating, stimulating, exciting, revitalizing, energizing, vitalizing, thrilling, stirring, inspiring, uplifting, delighting.

***ex*otic**
strikingly unusual or different; unique, novel, singular, striking, impressive, extraordinary, fantastic, remarkable, marvelous, glamorous, colorful.

***ex*perienced**
skilled or learned through practice; practiced, accomplished, proficient, skillful, adept, prepared, ready, versed, knowledgeable, competent, capable, able, efficient, professional, good, expert, master, masterly, savvy, sophisticated, worldly, wise.

***ex*pert**
characterized by a high degree of skill or knowledge; proficient, adept, masterful, skillful, master, professional, polished, practiced, accomplished, experienced, adroit, deft, facile, knowledgeable, learned, well-versed, well-informed.

***ex*pressive**
conveying meaning or feeling; eloquent, emotive, emotional, passionate, intense.

***ex*quisite**
1. having a particular beauty, charm or refinement; beautiful, attractive, striking, handsome, elegant, refined, graceful, delicate. **2.** characterized by great excellence; fine, excellent, rare, precious, choice, superior, select, splendid, outstanding, matchless, incomparable.

***ex*traordinary**
beyond what is usual, ordinary or customary; unusual, remarkable, rare, exceptional, singular, unique, special, invaluable, surprising, striking, amazing, phenomenal, astonishing, wondrous, fantastic, fabulous, majestic, prodigious, august, important, eminent, notable.

***ex*troverted**
having an outgoing personality; sociable, gregarious, friendly, congenial, amiable.

***ex*uberant**
marked by good health and high spirits; high-spirited, vivacious, ebullient, sparkling, effervescent, zesty, buoyant, lively, animated, enthusiastic, energetic.

xenodochial
open and receptive to strangers or foreigners; hospitable, friendly, benign, warm, sociable, amiable, pleasant, congenial, cordial, polite, courteous, gracious, liberal, broad-minded, unprejudiced, unbiased: *The xenodochial tour guide was in the right business*

Y

yare
moving quickly and easily; nimble, lithe, well-coordinated, agile, active, deft, lively, brisk, facile, spry, quick, swift, fast, fleet, speedy: *Ron's yare response saved the sail from being swept overboard.*

yeomanly
marked by loyalty and allegiance; loyal, faithful, devoted, dedicated, allegiant, patriotic, true-blue, true, steadfast, staunch, fast, unwavering.

yielding
showing courteous submission or respect; accommodating, obliging, amenable, agreeable, deferential, respectful, polite, thoughtful, obeisant, courteous.

young
having the qualities or appearance of youth; youthful, vigorous, active, fresh, keen, enthusiastic, optimistic, hopeful, confident, cheerful, light-hearted, bright-eyed, buoyant, yeasty, naive, innocent.

youthful
marked by the qualities of youth; young, active, vigorous, fresh, enthusiastic, sanguine, optimistic, hopeful, cheerful, buoyant, yeasty, light-hearted, innocent.

Z

zany
whimsically comical; laughable, amusing, comic, risible, silly, gay, hilarious, merry, mirthful, jocund, jovial, playful, frolicsome, sportive.

zealous
marked by intense enthusiasm or desire; keen, eager, earnest, ardent, fervid, fervent, enthusiastic, excited, passionate, impassioned, intense, devoted, devout.

zestful
characterized by hearty enjoyment or excitement; zesty, vibrant, alive, vivacious, energetic, lively, dynamic, animated, enthusiastic, exuberant, excited, ebullient, jovial, cheerful, blithe, sparkling, chipper, jaunty, buoyant, sprightly, playful, frisky, frolicsome, hearty, yeasty.

zingy
marked by vitality and enthusiasm; vital, animated, energetic, lively, enthusiastic, exuberant, zesty, vivacious, spirited.

zippy
full of life and energy; lively, peppy, alive, spry, active, sprightly, bouncy, breezy, frisky, vigorous, dynamic, energetic: *The sound of Bill's zippy step announced his arrival.*

PART II

THE ART OF APPRECIATION

WHAT IS APPRECIATION?

Next to physical survival, the greatest need of a human being is psychological survival—to be understood, to be affirmed, to be validated, to be appreciated Stephen Covey

The dictionary defines appreciation as *that which recognizes the quality or significance of; that which admires greatly, that which values.* When we appreciate others, when we acknowledge and affirm ourselves, we are recognizing that each of us is significant in this world, that each of our lives is valuable. Appreciation is not false praise. Nor is it manipulation. It is the sincere and specific recognition and affirmation of the qualities that are unique to each of us. Appreciation builds our self-esteem and propels us toward accomplishing our positive goals and making meaningful contributions. In the following pages I'll discuss both the power of receiving appreciation and the value of expressing appreciation. First I want to discuss what appreciation is composed of.

Appreciation has two components: recognition and expression. While it begins with recognition, appreciation completes itself through expression—acknowledgment. A few years ago I had an opportunity to work with a group of six-year-old children—not my usual audience. The program I did for them was part of an ongoing art series at the Pacific Art Center in Seattle. Entitled *Mirror, Mirror On the Wall*, the focus of my program was to combine self-esteem with art by having the children paint their names on T-shirts and create esteeming acronyms for their names using words from *The Loving Dictionary*.

I had printed words from the book on colorful flash cards which I placed randomly around the room. We didn't talk about self-esteem. We just talked about the words and what they meant. For instance, as they were painting their names, we talked about how they were using their *imagination* and being *creative*. When they ran to greet their moms or dads, they were being *active* and *energetic.* When they were learning to read they were using their *intelligence*. I asked them how it felt when someone told them good things about themselves. The consensus, in Tony the Tiger's word: *Grrreat!* Even though they couldn't pronounce all of the words, they recognized the letters that matched their names and identified with the qualities that we discussed.

ALICE chose the words Active, Likable, Imaginative, Cute, and Energetic to describe herself. She told me she was active because she could run and jump. She was imaginative because she thought up good games. JOHN chose Jolly, Original, Honest, Nice. He said he liked to laugh, and that he was honest because when he lost his brother's softball, he told his dad.

The words had a lot of impact on the children. They were vibrant and engaged and totally cooperative. They went out of their way to help each other find words that matched their names, and they joyfully shared their colors and sparkles while painting. It was as though all competition melted away as each child was recognized and filled with appreciation for her or his own uniqueness.

At the beginning of the program, the mother of one of the boys had apologized to me, explaining that her son always got antsy after awhile and would want to leave early. Much to her surprise, he was the last to leave. Another mother later told me why she had enrolled her daughter. The previous week she had asked her daughter to tell her three things she liked about herself and her daughter couldn't think of anything.

This woman felt very concerned because she considers herself to be a good mother. She tells her daughter how much she loves her, and she kisses and hugs her. What she realized, though, was that if she did not *tell* her daughter—express to her—how *generous, kind,* and *intelligent* she was when she demonstrated those qualities, there was no way for her daughter to know or to recognize those good things about herself.

We can experience great love and appreciation, even great admiration for people, but unless we consciously express that appreciation to them directly, it has no value. Appreciation needs to move from thoughts and feelings to expression—to specific acknowledgment of all the good things we think and feel. With appreciation we know when we've done something right; when we've behaved in a way that has enriched another person's life; when we've demonstrated a quality that we can use for good.

Appreciation is the greatest gift we can give to another human being, because it satisfies a basic psychological need—to be seen and affirmed. I've met many successful people with what could be called *average* intelligence or talents, who excelled because they were taught to believe in themselves. I've also met people with what could be called *average* looks, who radiated beauty and charisma because they had been taught to value themselves. It was the acknowledgment of others that enabled these people to recognize, appreciate and cultivate their unique qualities and strengths.

While it is important to understand the significance of appreciation, it is equally important to understand that appreciation is *not* manipulation. Genuine appreciation has no strings attached. False appreciation manipulates. Any praise, compliment or appreciation that is expressed with the intention of getting someone to do something or to improve performance can be interpreted as manipulation. While it might provide short-term motivation, over time trust can dissolve and the appreciation can become meaningless. In order for appreciation to be received fully and to have a meaningful impact, it needs to be expressed with the sole purpose of enriching the life of the other person.

THE POWER OF RECEIVING APPRECIATION

There is more hunger for love and appreciation in this world than for bread. Mother Teresa

If you're like the majority of people I know, including myself, you'd love to have more appreciation in your life—to have someone recognize you, admire you, acknowledge you for being *honest, capable, lovable, courageous,* or *deserving.*

So if we want more appreciation, why do we reject compliments? Someone tells us we look nice and we so often respond with "No, I don't," or "Not really." Why do we close our minds and hearts to the very appreciation that, in many cases, we hunger for? Frequently I'm asked, "Is it because I don't feel good about myself?" From my perspective the answer is that we don't know how to *recognize* the good in ourselves. We can't know what we don't know until we know it!

How do we learn to recognize the good things in ourselves? The same way we've learned to identify our shortcomings—by someone at some time telling us.

According to the National Council for Self-Esteem, the average adult in our country can identify six weaknesses for every strength. The reason? The greater majority of feedback we've heard has been negative. Though a lot has been well-intentioned, correctional feedback, it hasn't been balanced with an equal amount of positive, loving feedback. As a result, we have a national deficit of positive self-knowledge which can undermine our human resourcefulness and our morale. *They never see what I do right, only what I do wrong* is the familiar lament heard in homes, schools and offices.

So it's no surprise to me that we reject compliments. Like computers, our brains are designed to receive, process and store information. If you've ever tried to open a file in your computer and got the message *This file cannot be opened because the program cannot be found…*Bingo! That is what's happening in our brains when we receive a compliment that doesn't have a matching program. We cannot open to receive it.

To compensate for the missing programs, most of us have developed interesting techniques for processing compliments. I have affectionately dubbed the three most common techniques *The Benihana, The*

Complimentary Ping-Pong and *The Doubting Thomas*. We know them well.

The Benihana is named after the knife-wielding chefs at the famous Japanese restaurants who expertly slice and dice our food into tiny bits right before our very eyes. Who hasn't given someone a compliment like, "You did a great job on that presentation," only to hear, "No, I didn't. I screwed up. I missed one of my key points." The compliment, sliced and diced into tiny bits right before our eyes.

The Complimentary Ping-Pong requires two players. We've probably all heard it. *Ping*: "You did a great job on that report." *Pong*: "Oh, no, you're the one who did most of the work." *Ping*: "No, I just filled in the missing pieces." *Pong*: "But, you're the one who did it." The compliments, flying back and forth, never score for either player.

And finally, the familiar sounds of *The Doubting Thomas*: "You did a great job!" The usual response if only in thought: "Oh, yeah! Whatdyawant?!"

I understand that inexperience in receiving appreciation, praise or compliments can create discomfort—everything from sweaty palms and red faces to shortness of breath. There was a time in my life when I thought something was wrong with me because I didn't know how to receive appreciation. It was as though a part of me was missing. When people praised or complimented me, I didn't know how to respond. I heard the words but they never got into my heart. Consequently, I discounted a lot of the good things that happened to me.

It took awareness and practice: awareness that I didn't know how to receive the appreciation, and practice to create new programs and belief systems that would allow me to receive it. Learning to receive appreciation is a process, and it's important to be patient and kind with yourself along the way. Like learning to ride a bike, it may be unfamiliar and uncomfortable at first, but when you get the hang of it, you'll always remember it! And it can free you to enjoy your successes.

So practice. If we want more appreciation, we need to take responsibility for opening "new files" to receive it. If you can, look the other person in the eye and accept their gift of appreciation by simply saying *Thank you*. Take a deep breath. When we breathe, we expand. We begin to make room for receiving the appreciation and creating new programs. If you're inclined, let the other person know that you're learning to receive appreciation and that you could be more comfortable.

By your example, you will give them permission to receive appreciation too.

Even if you *could have* done better on a particular presentation or job or whatever, instead of beating yourself up or rejecting the compliment, mentally review what you would have done differently and say *Thank you.* Cut yourself some slack. It's taken me a long time to recognize that even when I'm not functioning at 100%, my efforts still have value. Give yourself permission to receive the praise and appreciation for everything that you *did* accomplish. The more you practice, the more comfortable you'll be with receiving appreciation.

When there are two or more people responsible for the success of a project, the same rules apply. STOP and take a breath. Take a few seconds to let whatever appreciation is being expressed to you sink in. Say *Thank you.* Then you can express your appreciation to the other person who shares your success.

It is also vital to realize that when someone compliments us for a quality or trait that we don't yet recognize in ourselves, it doesn't mean we don't possess that trait.

When I was in school, I had a part-time job with a national merchandising company. The company was in the process of converting all of their data to computers. My job was to categorize information that had been compiled on endless reams of paper. One day when I came to work, there were three chairs lined up in front of my desk. I gulped, fearing that I was about to be fired. Instead, it turned out that the chairs were there for three efficiency experts. They wanted to study how I worked because I was processing the information at a much faster rate than anyone else in the department. I wasn't competing with anyone, I was simply using a skill I didn't even know I had.

They labeled my work as *organized* and *efficient*, words I had never heard about myself before! Based on my organizing process, they created a model for others to follow that enabled them to process the information more efficiently. Ever since then I have learned to pay attention to and value my gift for organization. Many times over the years, in both my personal and professional life, when I have felt overwhelmed with what seemed like endless details, their gift of recognition to me for being *organized* and *efficient* has enabled me to trust in my ability to organize and handle the details.

Note that the recognition—the appreciation—was attached to a specific behavior, so I was able to trust in it and take it in. If you're doubtful or confused about any appreciation that is being expressed to you, you can actually help others express their appreciation more fully. You can ask them to identify exactly what it was that you did or said that stimulated their response.

For example, if someone acknowledges you for doing a *great job* and you're not sure exactly what they mean, ask them to identify exactly what you did right. Was it what you said or how you said it? Was it the information in the report that helped them, or was it getting the task completed on time?

Or maybe someone calls you *handsome*. If you've never been called *handsome* before or you're uncomfortable, you can ask them what they find handsome or attractive about you. Is it the color of your eyes, the shape of your face, your hair? I know this is a new way of receiving appreciation that can stretch your comfort zones. Experiment. I have found that people *like* to elaborate, to appreciate.

Good job can mean many things to many people. And *handsome* or *beautiful* can encompass all forms of beauty, not just what we see on magazine covers. By asking for specifics you get to experience receiving their appreciation more fully and they get to experience expressing it more fully. If they question your asking or wonder if you're fishing for more compliments, tell them it's important information that will help you to duplicate your efforts in the future or understand what they enjoy about you.

When someone gives you a compliment and you're able to receive it, notice how they respond. I've heard it said that you can tell a person's character by the way praise is received. When you open to receive praise, you also receive respect.

THE VALUE OF EXPRESSING APPRECIATION

Accurate, perceptive praise is a rarity in our society. It shouldn't be. We all need it and we all love to give it. It's just that nobody ever told us it was okay. Barbara Sher

Recently I got a call from Dave, a graduate of one of my training programs. By his own admission, Dave is "not a feely touchy kind of guy." Yet one day after a session in which he had experienced both receiving and expressing appreciation, he decided to call a friend of his who was on the verge of losing his business and also going through a divorce.

Dave wanted to let his friend know how much he really appreciated him and how much he valued all the things they had shared over the years. However, when it came time to make the call, he couldn't bring himself to do it. He said he was uncomfortable and thought it would just embarrass his friend. But the situation nagged at him, so he decided to write a short note to his friend and send it instead. Then it took him a week to mail it.

Dave had called me to say he'd gotten a message on his voice mail from his friend. In tears the friend had thanked him, saying that it was the first time in over a year he had heard one good word about himself. Dave, *the not so feely touchy kind of guy*, was deeply touched—choked up—and very glad that he'd sent the note.

Mark Twain said, "I can live for two months on a good compliment." We may never even know how much the appreciation we express means to someone. Appreciation doesn't cost anything; lack of appreciation does. It is one of the leading reasons for employee turnover, customer dissatisfaction and divorce in our country. As Mother Teresa said, "If we want a love message to be heard, it has to be sent out—to keep a lamp burning we have to keep putting oil in it." We cannot expect any of our relationships, professional or personal, to thrive without consistent nurturing.

I'm fascinated that we never question the need for regular maintenance of our homes, cars or clothes. It's a given. If we don't take care of them they fall apart, break down or wear out. Yet when it comes to our relationships—to the precious, irreplaceable people in our lives—we tend to overlook their needs for regular attention and recognition.

But they know how I feel. No, they don't! Not unless you tell them. So take a moment and think of the people that you know. How many of them could use a few words of appreciation—accurate, perceptive praise for the ways they have enriched your life? Think of your family and friends, the people you work with, your neighbors. When was the last time you acknowledged them, either verbally or in writing, for something that you value and appreciate about them?

When I was in grade school I had a teacher who, like many well-intentioned people, could always find the one thing wrong with any project or homework assignment. Her class was not a lot of fun for me. My grades, no matter what I did, were average. By comparison, my eighth grade teacher, Sister Grace Patricia, had a very different approach. With all of her students she was firm and direct, but she lived the principle: *Catch them doing something right.* That year Sister Grace caught me doing a lot of things right, as well as a few things wrong, but she just knew how to keep a balance.

Under her tutelage I blossomed from a shy and mediocre student into an almost precocious girl who graduated with honors. I sang in the choir and actually had the courage to sing a solo at Christmas. For the first time in my life, I had a sense of confidence, a sense of my own power. Sister Grace was one of the first people I knew to appreciate me, to *recognize* and verbally acknowledge the good things in me. She was my cheerleader. Her appreciation changed my life.

With respect to my family and all the families that were raised under the yoke of humility, I know they did the best they could with what they knew. They did not know about the value of appreciation. They did not know how to be cheerleaders.

We all need cheerleaders and we all need to learn how to be cheerleaders. Can you imagine our professional football, basketball, or baseball teams without fans to cheer them on? Recognition is the name of the game whether we're on a playing field, in a corporate environment, at school or at home.

In order to be wholesome and enriching, appreciation needs to be anchored to positive behavior. There is a convicted murderer on death row who had been told since childhood *You can do anything.* And she did! Without being linked to positive values, the encouragement didn't serve anyone in the end. When we express appreciation, we need to *recognize* the positive behavior or quality that was demonstrated, and then we need to tell people *how* that behavior or quality enriched our lives or the lives of others.

For example, you might appreciate someone for a kindness extended that gave you a sense of belonging, of connection; for a talent that made you laugh and lifted your spirits; for a task well done and completed on time that added to your peace of mind. Understanding *why* we are being praised is an important component to the expression of appreciation.

This follows the model for expressing appreciation developed by Dr. Marshall B. Rosenberg, author of *Nonviolent Communication (NVC), A Language of Compassion.* The *NVC* way of expressing appreciation has these three components: this is what you did; this is how I feel about what you did; this is the need of mine that was met by what you did. It's pretty easy to use, even for people who don't like *that feely touchy stuff.*

Generally we use abbreviated forms of appreciation such as *That was kind of you. NVC* takes it further and deeper. *That was kind of you. When you offered to drop off that package for me, I felt relieved because I needed more time. When you offered to drop off that package*—what was done; *I felt relieved*—how you felt about what was done; *I needed more time*—what need of yours was met or satisfied by what was done.

This language is straightforward, simple *and* empowering. If you prefer, you can substitute the word *was* for *felt—I was relieved.* Just stating the feeling *relieved* conveys the same message and, in some professional situations, can be more impactful than using the expression *I feel.*

Whether we express appreciation in the abbreviated form or using the *NVC* model, the most important element is…expressing it. William James said, "The deepest principle in human nature is the craving to be appreciated." Expressing genuine appreciation to the people in our lives only takes a few moments. So do it! Not later…now!

When we express our appreciation to people, we unleash a powerful energy in them for good. Several years ago the ABC television show *20/20* featured a story about the Montreux Counseling Centre in Victoria, British Columbia. Specializing in the treatment of eating disorders, Montreux has succeeded where other treatment centers have failed. Suffering from bolemia or anorexia, many of their patients wind up there as a "last resort" after being told by other authorities that "nothing could be done for them."

In addition to all of the traditional therapies, Montreux has adopted an entirely positive approach to the treatment of these eating disorders. A critical first step they take with their patients is to establish an *unconditionally supportive environment.* One way they do that is by giving their patients positive verbal affirmation morning, noon and night. In essence, they *feed* their patients a steady diet of appreciation. Pay attention to the language in this statement from their brochure. It is a key to their success.

> *We have deep respect for the high sensitivity, creative intelligence, and individuality of each of the hundreds of "eating disorder" victims we have had the privilege to know and help during the past 10 years. We, as a society, must come to a more profound understanding of the special needs and gifts which these precious individuals present.*

At Montreux they have learned to recognize the uniqueness of each individual. They have learned to look beyond the surface, beyond the labels that distort our vision of one another. And with their words of recognition and appreciation, they have generated profound healing. Recidivism is low and many of their patients have gone on to become accomplished professionals in such diverse fields as art, health care and social science.

THE PURPOSE OF SELF-APPRECIATION

Definition of Self-Esteem: Appreciating my own worth and importance and having the character to be accountable for myself and to act responsibly toward others. National Council for Self-Esteem

Self-appreciation is the key to self-esteem. Self-appreciation is not about arrogance or lack of humility. Arrogance is an overcompensation for a lack of self-esteem, for self-doubt. True humility is, in fact, recognizing our gifts with gratitude and using them for our good and the good of others. Self-appreciation is about knowledge and trust. The more we learn to recognize and to value our strengths and good qualities, the more we learn to trust in ourselves, and the more others also trust us.

In her book *Feel The Fear And Do It Anyway*, Dr. Susan Jeffers states, "Security is not having things, it's handling things." When we trust in ourselves to handle things, no one can take our power away. Having enough trust in our abilities to respond to and handle what happens to us is what I call *respons-ability!* Being responsible requires knowing ourselves well enough to trust ourselves.

Self-trust and self-knowledge are so vital to our self-esteem that, when I coach one-on-one, I ask my clients to commit to a daily exercise that I call *One-A-Days*, vitamins of appreciation. Every day for the first three weeks that we work together, I ask them to identify one good quality they possess, to identify some action they took that demonstrated that quality, and then to state how taking that action made them feel and what need it satisfied. For instance, *I'm honest. Last week the cashier overlooked an item and I brought it to his attention. I felt good because I have a need for honesty in my life.*

This simple exercise can educate us about ourselves. It teaches us to *recognize* our good qualities and to anchor them to good deeds so we can believe and trust in ourselves. Though it is a simple exercise, for many people, it's hard to do.

When I started working with Michael, a successful realtor, he was at the top of his field. As the saying goes, he had it all—the house, the office, the car, the clothes and the family. Everyone admired and respected his accomplishments—everyone except Michael.

Like nearly 70% of the successful people in our country, Michael doubted that his success was real. It's what Dr. Pauline Rose Clance calls "The Impostor Phenomenon" in her book by the same name. Constantly restless, he was on the treadmill of *more, more, next, next!* He added to his house, expanded his office, bought a new car every year and a new wardrobe of clothes. The more he earned, the more he spent.

Driven by self-doubt, Michael came to me hoping to learn how to trust in himself and how to enjoy his successes. The first time I introduced him to *One-A-Days*, he laughed. He was very skeptical that it could make a difference and he was uncomfortable. I asked him just to do the exercise. By our next session, he wasn't laughing.

Michael acknowledged how hard it was for him to identify his good qualities, how hard it was to *believe* and *trust* in himself, to trust that his success wasn't just dumb luck, to accept that he was responsible for his success.

With time and consistent recognition of all the qualities that contributed to his success, Michael's trust in himself solidified. He now studies and celebrates his successes, acknowledging the qualities that created them, his *intelligence, patience* and *experience*. Michael studies his mistakes and set-backs as well. He notes what needs to be changed and moves on. And he's become a lot more forgiving of himself.

More grounded and centered, Michael is no longer driven by self-doubt. This past year his sales almost doubled. Most importantly, the quality of his life has improved dramatically. He's content with his three-year-old car, adds only the items that he really wants to his wardrobe, is managing his money better, has relative peace of mind and a healthier relationship with his family. A perfect life? No. More balanced, peaceful and connected? Yes. And learning how to appreciate himself was an essential key.

Another client of mine Ruth, sixty years of age and an accomplished professional, had been sensitive to criticism her whole life, especially from her family. After a steady diet of *One-a-Days* she reported that she was rarely getting hooked by the criticism.

She had begun to recognize—to appreciate—herself from the inside out and was far less susceptible to what other people said to her. She also noticed that the less susceptible she was, the less criticism came her way. And the more she appreciated herself, the more appreciation she received from others.

Mark Victor Hansen, co-author of the *Chicken Soup for the Soul* series, tells the following story. Years ago he experienced a financial crisis that left him almost broke. Notice he didn't say *poor*. To Mark the word *broke* means without money. The word *poor* means without resources.

Though he was scared, he knew and trusted in his own abilities—in his *intelligence, resilience, talent, imagination, determination,* and *professionalism.* He knew he was not without resources. He knew he would recover. And he did—big time! Without this self-knowledge of his positive qualities, he might well have floundered.

Self-knowledge deserves at least as much attention as we put into learning math and the sciences, literature and art. As with any other subject, the more we learn about our positive qualities the more confident we are to use them for our good, and the more respectful and appreciative we become of ourselves.

Last year I had the opportunity to visit the Salvador Dali Museum in Tampa, Florida. Though not among my favorite artists, Dali's style has always intrigued me. The docent who guided my tour, a retired art professor, was extremely knowledgeable and passionate about Dali and his work. With each new painting we explored, he provided information and insights that opened my eyes to Dali's genius. I left a Dali convert.

Knowledge had imbued me with respect and appreciation. Self-knowledge does the same. It imbues us with the appreciation, trust and self-confidence that builds our self-esteem.

THE IMPACT OF LABELS

Treat a man as he is and he will remain as he is. Treat a man as he can and should be and he will become as he can and should be. Goethe

A few years ago, I met a man in New York who works with students who would normally be labeled "at risk." However, he refuses to let anyone refer to them by that label. He calls them his "at promise" students. If you were one of his students, which label would you rather wear—and why? What's the big deal about a single word or label?

The big deal is that our words have the power to affect our self-image and to create a lifetime of either success or failure. This is how it works: neuroscientists recognize that our words, whether thought or spoken, are physical energy—electrochemical triggers or impulses that program the mind-body system with pictures and verbal commands. To experience the energy of your own words you can use the WORDpower™ Arm Exercise at the beginning of Part III.

When we tell a child *Don't spill the milk*, they still *spill the milk* because the words create a picture of spilling the milk. Even though the ear hears the word *Don't*, the brain receives the word picture of *spill the milk.* When we say instead *Keep the milk in the glass*, we create a word picture in the brain of the behavior that we do want.

When we label people as *lazy, insensitive* or *stubborn*, they get the picture of that negative label in their brains, and it becomes the model for their behavior. They also get the negative energy of the label, better known as "bad vibes."

Have you ever been around someone who didn't hold you in their highest esteem; who had a negative label of judgment on you? You can't win, can you? Because once that label is in their mind, you can do nine out of ten things right, but the negative label discounts all nine. They simply don't see the good things. As an ancient Chinese proverb says *Where the mind goes, the energy flows*. Do the one thing wrong that matches that negative label and of course they catch it.

When we use positive labels such as *helpful, sensitive* or *flexible*, the same process unfolds. The label creates a picture in people's minds and becomes an image for positive behavior. Plus others get our "good vibes."

The parents of a teenage girl shared with me their first-hand experience of the power of labeling. When their daughter did not want to help with chores, the mother would label her as *lazy*. Consequently, she couldn't get her daughter to help her with anything.

On the other hand, when the teenager did help with the chores, her father would affirm her as *helpful.* He would also let her know that he felt more relaxed with her support. He let her know *how* her behavior enriched his life. *Most often* when he needed help with something, guess how the daughter responded? *Helpfully.* One teenager—two different labels, two different behaviors. If someone called me *lazy* I would not be motivated to be *helpful*.

I know it could be a lot easier to refrain from judging and using negative labels when we're upset with someone. One of the best ways I've discovered to shift the energy of a negative label is to restate it with a positive label. For instance, if I'm labeling someone, either mentally or verbally, as *lazy* I'll restate it as s/he *could be more helpful at times*. I call this reframing. The words *could be* imply the possibility for change. The words *more helpful* shift my energy and create pictures in my mind for the positive behavior I do want. The words *at times* help me to keep things in perspective.

According to Dr. Marshall Rosenberg, the reason we judge is because we are not getting our needs met. For example, if I need a hug from someone and I don't ask for it, chances are I won't get it. When I don't get the hug, I might wind up judging that person as *cold* or *insensitive*. Consciously or unconsciously, when we label people, we judge them, and when we judge them we set up an expectation in our own minds for their behavior that becomes a self-fulfilling prophesy.

In a well-known computer mix up, a class of *bright* students was mislabeled *dumb* and a class of supposedly *dumb* students was mislabeled *bright*. The teachers believed the labels and proceeded to teach their classes according to the labels. Five and a half months later, they discovered the mistake and tested the students. The IQ test points of the *bright* students had gone down significantly while the test points of the supposedly *dumb* students had gone up.

Last year a group I trained was having difficulty with a supervisor whom everyone had labeled for a long time as *negative* and *close-minded.* I asked them to join in an experiment: replacing the negative labels with positive labels that indicated the behavior they wanted from the supervisor, in this case—*open-minded* and *supportive*.

I instructed them to replace the negative labels in both their thoughts and discussions of the supervisor with the positive labels (to the best of their ability) for at least three weeks. For example: *He could be more open-minded and supportive*. I also asked them to identify any good quality the supervisor displayed and to verbally acknowledge it to both the supervisor and in conversation among themselves.

They had already done the WORDpower™ Arm Exercise and had experienced that when they used the negative labels they lost energy, and when they used the positive labels they gained energy. So even though they were very doubtful about this experiment, they were willing and frustrated enough to give it a try. (The very first thing they noticed was that every time one of them used a positive label about the supervisor, the thought of the supervisor behaving in that manner was so far-fetched, it made them laugh.)

As the three-week experiment came to a close, the supervisor called a meeting to ask for input on some new changes that were being implemented at the site. It was the first time he had demonstrated being *open* to input from others! *Where the mind goes, the energy flows.*

Not every negative behavior or attitude will be corrected by reframing the label, but by doing so we can stop a negative label from becoming a negative pattern. Tony DiCicco, coach of the World Cup-winning U.S. Women's Soccer Team believes in "coaching positive." He doesn't overlook the things that need to be improved or changed. But if a goal is missed, he analyzes the situation and uses humor to correct. By developing our own skills at coaching positive, we can learn to look for and to cultivate the very best in people. In his best-selling book *Raising Positive Kids in a Negative World*, Zig Ziglar makes the following astute observation.

> *It is true that everyone can't excel in all areas, such as brains, brawn, or good looks, but you can assure your child that he can be just as honest, courteous, cheerful, loyal, faithful, enthusiastic, and any one of a hundred other positive things as others are. Those are qualities he can take to the marriage or business marketplace and find ready buyers.*

I believe that if kids were taught to recognize and appreciate more of the positive qualities they each possess, they would have less need for defining themselves with designer labels.

We also need to stay aware of the words we choose to label ourselves. Whether positive or negative, the labels we choose tell others how to treat us. Just as self-appreciation cultivates respect, negative labels such as *dummy, klutz* or *disorganized* diminish respect. Stop using negative labels on yourself, even jokingly. Speak of yourself the way you would have others treat you. *I learn quickly* or *I could be more knowledgeable about that topic.*

While I applaud and support the extraordinary work of the Twelve-Step recovery programs, I strongly advise that each individual stay aware of the *prolonged* use of negative labels such as *dysfunctional, abused, victimized, alcoholic.* While such labels can be accurate, they speak of past experiences. There is a time to unveil and shed light on those dark experiences, and there is a time to let them go.

When the time is right for us, we can graduate to speaking of the past in more proactive terms. For example, *I had an abusive childhood but I had the courage and resiliency to move beyond that by creating new patterns in my life*. Or you could choose language such as *I could have had a more loving, respectful, nurturing, playful, safer childhood.* The new labels help us to release the past and to fill our minds with the healing we do want. If we had an abscessed wound, it would need to be lanced and tended in order for it to heal. If we kept scratching at it, it would never heal. If you're unsure of how your choice of labels is affecting you, experiment with the WORDpower™ Arm Exercise.

THE TIME FOR APPRECIATION IS NOW

When he was on his deathbed the Duke of Ellington was asked if he would have lived his life differently. He answered: *I would give more praise.*

We can begin bettering our world by starting where we have the most impact—people within arm's reach, within the sound of our voice or the sight of our eyes. The three major environments where we can cultivate appreciation are at home, school and work, the places where we spend most of our lives.

Without placing judgment on yourself, pay attention today to how often you tend to correct or criticize versus appreciate and praise. Do you lift and encourage? If not, why not? Old habits can be changed with a bit of awareness. And, yes, there is time, and the time is now!

Begin at home. As you rush to get the kids off to school or get yourself to work, STOP! Take fifteen seconds to look into your child's eyes or your mate's eyes or your own and connect. Connection—being seen and heard—is a valuable form of appreciation. Tell them "Thanks for putting the cap on the toothpaste," or "I love you," or "I think you're great," or whatever is current. It's when we're the busiest that we need appreciation and connection the most!

Turn the television and the computer off! And have dinner together. Take a few minutes while eating to acknowledge everything that you've accomplished that day—family brag time—or even to ask for appreciation.

My mom had a great way of connecting with us at dinner and getting appreciation. After working all day, she'd come home and prepare dinner. If my brother Bill and I didn't say anything about the meal, she'd start a conversation with herself: *Well, Julie that was a really fine spaghetti sauce you made. Thank you, Julie. How did you make that?* and so on. My brother and I would look at each other, take the cue and proceed to thank her and compliment her for what a wonderful meal she'd made.

At school remember that appreciation is a two way street. Whether you're the student, teacher or principal, if you want others to *catch you doing something right*, then start by *catching them doing something right*. Everyone needs a steady diet of appreciation.

Be spontaneous. If you think it—say it! It only takes a few moments. It's the unexpected moments of appreciation and connection that bring the greatest satisfaction. Pay attention not only to how you feel when you express appreciation to others, but also to what impact it has on them.

Allow yourself to be creative. There are many ways to express appreciation and connect with people. A principal of a middle school in Oregon makes a point of knowing the names of every one of the 800 students in his school. New students are surprised and elated when, after only a few weeks at school, he calls them by name. They feel seen, recognized and welcomed by him.

At work look for everything that is being accomplished or that has been done. Take thirty seconds to acknowledge people for their accomplishments—to connect with them and say *thanks*. You can say it by email, voice mail or post-it notes. You can say it privately if that suits their style, or publicly. You can say it with food like pizza and cookies or by scheduling fun activities.

I worked with an international food company for two years, training their sales teams. The members of each regional team were brought together at a hotel each year for a week of training. In addition to the training sessions, the company scheduled free time and activities such as plays, sporting events and boat rides during the week.

At the end of the week those who attended filled out company evaluations. I was impressed with the consistent responses to one question: "What was the most valuable part of this week for you?" The uniform response: *Their time together to connect and have fun.* Because the company made time for their personal needs, the team members felt valued and appreciated.

Another Chinese proverb says *A bit of fragrance always clings to the hand that gives you roses*. When we look for the good in others, we find the good in ourselves. When we find the good in ourselves, we become a powerful force for good in the world. Start now. This is your *Loving Dictionary* and your life. I guarantee you that there is at least one person you know who needs to hear something good about themselves—today!

PART III

CREATIVE WAYS TO EXPRESS APPRECIATION

A WHY-NOT BOOK

Why should good words ne'er be said of a friend till he is dead. Daniel Webster Hoyt

The Loving Dictionary is not a how-to book. It is a why-not book. Why not use it lovingly, wisely—and often? To support you in doing just that I've listed a host of easy, creative ways to use the words in this book along with some fun word games. They have all worked great for me, both in my professional and personal life. Please write and tell me how you've used *The Loving Dictionary* to enrich your life or that of another. If you create a new way to express appreciation, let me know. I'll include it in later editions.

THE WORDpower™ ARM EXERCISE

Think before thou speakest. Cervantes

To demonstrate the powerful physical energy of your words, use this simple arm exercise. *(Refrain from doing this exercise if you have any injury or experience pain at any time during the exercise.)* This is a form of kinesiology, muscle testing. It only takes a minute. There are three steps.

- To do this exercise you need a partner. From a standing position, lift your strongest arm straight out to your side and comfortably up to shoulder level. Either speak or think of a positive label you have for someone else or for yourself. For instance, *S/he is so considerate*. Or *I'm very capable.* As you are stating the label, have your partner press down on your wrist using *just two fingers*. Resist the pressure. Notice your arm will stay strong and will not be able to be pushed down. The positive label is filling your entire mind-body system with its energy. When we use positive words, we feel empowered and energized.

- Then use a negative label such as *S/he is so insensitive*. Or *I'm such a klutz.* Have your partner apply pressure again. You will not be able to resist the pressure and hold your arm up. Your mind-body system is being affected adversely by the negative label. In this state of mind we lose our energy and feel powerless.

- To reclaim your energy and your power, restate or just think the positive label *S/he is so considerate.* Or *I'm very capable.* Reapply the pressure. Your arm will test strong. You may want to experiment with different words, just to prove this to yourself.

GIMME AN A™, THE WORD GAME

Words have a longer life than deeds. Pindar

Discover the good qualities in yourself and others. With Gimme An A™, a simple and fun word game, everyone's a winner! You can play it anytime, anywhere, with two or more people.

- *One player starts by asking the others in the group to* Gimme An A, *or a* B, *or any other letter of their choice from the alphabet. Let's use* B *for an example. The player who chooses the letter remains out of play to receive the appreciation.*

- *The other players respond with positive words starting with the chosen letter—in this case* B, *such as* brave, bold, bubbly—*that describe the good qualities of the player who chose the letter. Players can do this in any order and each player can respond with as many words as s/he can think of.*

- *When the group has used all the words that they can think of, then the next player chooses a letter and the next until everyone has had a turn.*

THE SWYTCH™

Great for parties, *The* Swytch™ is a fast-paced, competitive variation of Gimme An A™. Yet it still makes everybody a winner! Players will need *The Loving Dictionary*, a stopwatch, paper and pencils. The word game consists of rounds. The player to win the most rounds wins the game. The number of rounds is determined by the number of players to ensure that each player has had a chance to choose a letter and receive appreciation. But the number of rounds is not limited to the number of players. For example, with five players there will be at least five rounds. If there is a tie and two players have each won two rounds, play will continue until one player wins a third round.

- *A round begins with one player asking the others in the group to* Gimme An A, *or a* B, *or any other letter of their choice from the alphabet. Let's use* C *for an example. The player who chooses the letter remains out of play to receive the appreciation and to act as the timekeeper.*

- *Going clockwise, each player in the group has twenty seconds to respond with one positive word starting with the chosen letter—in this case* C, *such as* caring, creative, charitable*—that describes the good qualities of the player who chose the letter. As each player responds, s/he also writes down the words s/he has chosen.*

- *If a player cannot think of a word starting with the chosen letter, in this case* C, *s/he can make a* Swytch™ *by picking a synonym for the last word in use. For example, if the last adjective used is* charitable, *a* Swytch™ *could be made to one of its synonyms such as* generous. *There is no limit to the number of* Swytches™ *that can be made during a round.*

- *Once a* Swytch™ *has been made, the round continues with the players choosing words starting with the first letter of the synonym—in this case* G *for* generous*—such as* genial, gregarious, genuine.

- *If a word is chosen that has multiple meanings and the next player wants to make a* Swytch™, *s/he can choose a synonym for any one of its meanings. Let's use* bright *as an example.* Bright *can mean either* smart *or* lively. *Either synonym* smart *or* lively *could be used for a* Swytch™.

- *When players cannot think of either a word or a* Swytch™ *within the allotted time, they forfeit a turn but they can use the next twenty seconds of play to consult* The Loving Dictionary.

- *Once a word is used within a round, it cannot be used again within that round. Variations of a word can be used within the same round, such as* adventurous *and* adventuresome.

- *A round is won by the first player to accumulate five words. A new round begins with another player choosing a letter, then another until each player has had a turn. The player to win the most rounds is the winner of the game.*

THE ESTEEMING ACRONYM

Whether you think you can or you think you can't, you are right. Henry Ford

What's in a name? You and your self-image. So don't just sign your name. Design your name! This wonderful tool can be used in a variety of ways. Just match esteeming words from *The Loving Dictionary* to the name of any individual, school, team or business as a way of defining the good qualities they represent.

- Start by creating a powerful acronym using your own name. Take the letters of your first and last names. Attach esteeming words to them so that your name becomes a description of the real and positive you.

For example:

For example:	**M**agnificent	**J**oyful
	Attractive	**O**pen
	Resourceful	**N**atural
	Youthful	**E**legant
		Sincere

- Display your acronym where you'll see it often—on your desk or refrigerator, or inside your notebook, appointment book or medicine chest. Read it out loud with conviction. Have others repeat it back to you.
- Paint your acronym on a T-shirt or sweatshirt.
- Create business cards using the acronym.
- Make up a song using the qualities.

ONE-A-DAYS

Take inventory of the things you do well and praise yourself for those achievements and you build self-esteem. Wally "Famous" Amos

Give yourself a daily dose of appreciation. Every day for at least three weeks identify one good quality that you possess and some action you took that demonstrated that quality. Then state how taking that action made you feel and what need it satisfied. Here are some examples.

- *I'm resourceful. Last week the new computer system crashed. Instead of losing my cool, I found someone to repair it within the day at a reasonable price. I felt satisfied because I need order in my life and getting the computer fixed helped maintain that order.*

- *I'm patient and considerate. Yesterday, even though I was a few minutes late, I let another driver go ahead of me. I felt relieved because it affirmed I did have enough time. And I felt good because I want consideration in my life.*

- *I'm persevering. When I started to study Spanish, I barely knew how to say "hello." Even though I was really frustrated at times, I'm proud because I stuck with it. Now I have a pretty good vocabulary and I'm able to have a dialogue in Spanish. And I continue to practice.*

This simple exercise educates us about ourselves. It teaches us to *recognize* our good qualities and to anchor them to actions and deeds so we can believe and trust in ourselves.

DIAL-A-HEART

The applause of a single human being is of great consequence. Samuel Johnson

If you're having *one of those days*, give yourself a chance to vent your frustrations. Pick up the nearest phone and call a friend or loved one. Ask them if they have five or ten minutes to just listen. Relate your feelings and tell them what's going on. Then get back on track fast by asking them for a boost of loving words, *to tell you something good about yourself.* When they do, take a deep breath, relax and say *thank you.* Then hang up. Respect their time and energy, and yours.

TOUCH-A-HEART

Nobody has ever measured, even poets, how much the heart can hold. Zelda Fitzgerald

If you find yourself thinking good things about someone, tell them! Make that call. Ask them if they have one minute. Then give verbal expression to your thoughts and feelings about them. Be as descriptive as you can. Remember, every word of appreciation that you express to others spells *TLC* (tender loving care) and a boost of energy for both you and them. While the sound of a human voice transmits a lot of good energy, email can also do the job.

THE CHAMPION TAPE

Words are legions of metaphors that march through our minds. They...defend us, give us strength, and lead us to our victories. Shad Helmstetter

The Champion Tape is a powerful esteeming tool that you can use to celebrate and invigorate yourself and others.

- Celebrate all your good qualities. Record a tape of all your positive qualities. Make a long list, using as many synonyms as you can find. Add any qualities you desire to have, using language such as *I'm learning to be better organized* or *I'd like to be more confident.* Use affirmative phrases like *I am honest, I have confidence, I enjoy being responsible, I like, trust, appreciate myself!* Remember to incorporate the three components of appreciation from *Nonviolent Communication* found in Part II, "The Value of Expressing Appreciation." If, for any reason, using the words *I am* isn't comfortable for you yet, simply use the words *you are* instead. Or you can have someone you trust record the tape for you using the words *you are* and your name. The more affirmative phrases you use, the more powerful your tape will be. Action energizes your words, so play it often while exercising, driving or cleaning the house. Add music to the background for enhanced enjoyment.

- Make tapes for your children, loved ones, friends, and coworkers. Record them either alone or with a group of people. Use others' names and *you are* when telling them how you value and appreciate them. Surprise your family and friends with these tapes on special occasions such as going off to college, birthdays, anniversaries or promotions.

THE GIFT OF BLISS

Whatever kind of word thou speakest the like shall thou hear. Anonymous

I like to call this process *appreciation in stereo*. At The Center for Spiritual Living in Seattle, Senior Minister Kathianne Lewis uses a special process that she came upon some years ago. It's called *Giving Bliss*. One person stands or sits with two people, one on either side of them. The two people on either side simultaneously speak into the person's ears, verbalizing a steady stream of good things about that person. This is *giving bliss*. The two people giving the bliss keep this up for about two or three minutes. It's an awesome experience!

CREATE A UNIQUE SURPRISE PARTY

So is a word better than a gift. Holy Bible, Apocrypha

Create an *esteeming theme party* for birthdays and other occasions. Celebrate the individual by decorating banners, balloons, and cakes with all the positive qualities that they possess. Choose gifts that reflect those positive qualities. If it's your own birthday party, you can ask your guests to give you the gift of appreciation. Ask them to tell you something that they value about you. I've been doing this for years. It's an uplifting experience for everyone.

DECORATE AS YOU EDUCATE

I love to learn, but I hate to be taught. Winston Churchill

Paint words from *The Loving Dictionary* all over your child's room as a border, or do this in the classroom at day school, Sunday school or any school. Or just print them on colorful pieces of paper and put them around the room. As a child demonstrates the positive behavior and qualities of the words that are painted on the walls, point out the words. Talk to them about the words, about what they mean and how those words reflect their behavior. You can use this playful time together to teach them how to spell the words.

REKINDLE YOUR LOVE ON VALENTINE'S DAY

As long as one can admire and love, then one is young forever. Pablo Casals

For Valentine's Day, Abigail Van Buren of "Dear Abby" invites her readers to make a list of all the good qualities of their mates and to give it to them. Acknowledging all of his or her positive qualities is a very meaningful way to say *I love you.* It reawakens a lot of good memories. I suggest that you keep the list on hand and refer to it if you get upset with your partner. It will remind you of his or her good traits and why you chose your mate, and it will help restore good feelings.

BE THANKFUL AT THANKSGIVING

A word spoken in due season, how sweet it is! Holy Bible, Proverbs

Dr. Arthur Caliandro, senior minister at Marble Collegiate Church in New York City, celebrates Thanksgiving by remembering someone from his past who helped him or did something good for him—someone he forgot to thank. He locates them and writes them a letter or he calls them. It is very gratifying. I've been doing this now for about fifteen years. One year I contacted a woman who had been a guiding light for a period of time in my life. Within that following year she made her transition (my way of saying she died). I was very glad that I had taken the time to thank her and to let her know how her wisdom and guidance had contributed to my life.

DESIGN A DAY, WEEK OR MONTH OF APPRECIATION

Man lives more by affirmation than by bread. Victor Hugo

At home, school, or work designate a day, week or month to celebrate all of the positive qualities that the people around you possess. *Acknowledge everyone*—all the members of your family, all the students in your class or all the coworkers at your job. If you choose a day, acknowledge the positive qualities or behaviors that family members possess or exhibit, either in general, or during the course of that particular day. You can do it verbally or in writing. If you choose a week or month, you can designate each day within that week or month for a different quality. For example, you could dedicate days to appreciating *courage, perseverance, responsibility.* Or you can designate a different quality for each week or month. A week or month of *fairness, punctuality, competence.* Remember to *acknowledge everyone*.

EXPAND YOUR VOCABULARY OF APPRECIATION

The only way to speak the truth is to speak lovingly. Henry David Thoreau

Vitalize your self-expression with *The Loving Dictionary*, your personal resource for the language of appreciation. Use it for…

- thank you notes
- letters
- birthday and holiday greeting cards
- poetry
- class assignments
- evaluations
- esteeming love notes to be placed in a lunch box, pocket, or briefcase
- anonymous notes of appreciation to be placed on desks, lockers, or notebooks

THE ATTITUDE OF GRATITUDE

Heaviness in the heart of man maketh it stoop—but a good word maketh it glad. Holy Bible, Proverbs

- Be grateful for everything that you have accomplished. How many times have you gotten to the end of a long and productive day only to look back and focus on what you didn't accomplish? No matter what your job, take a few minutes and look back over your day. Acknowledge everything that you have done. Note any completion. Review the progress you made on any project. I've been self-employed for over twenty years. Often there's no one around to pat me on the back. By acknowledging myself for all that I have done I satisfy my own needs for appreciation, and that helps me to stay motivated.

- Giving thanks is a great way to relax. If you'd like to sleep better, try this. Before you go to sleep, take a few minutes to think about the good things that have happened to you during your day—a parking spot, a kind word from someone or the patience you exercised with your child or mate…or yourself! By filling you mind-body system with these thoughts, you will sleep better and wake feeling better too!

- Gratitude is a great balancing agent in times of adversity. If you're dealing with adversity, make a list of everything that is still right and good in your life. Reverends Karen Ludvig and Steve Towles are co-ministers of Seattle's Unity Church of Truth. They are also husband and wife. Several years ago, Karen's mother died. A short time later, only days after the family moved into a new house, Karen was stricken with an illness that almost claimed her life. Then their cat was killed by a wild animal and their dog was hit by a car. I remember Steve's sermon one Sunday on the heels of all these tragedies. He told us he had been so discouraged that he hadn't been able to see anything good in his life, so he forced himself to sit down and make a list of everything that was still right and good in his life and in his family's life. It worked, getting him to think in a different way, lifting his spirits and helping him to see the light at the end of the tunnel.

Keep my words positive, words become my behaviors
Keep my behaviors positive, behaviors become my habits
Keep my habits positive, habits become my values
Keep my values positive, values become my destiny.
Mahatma Gandhi

POSTSCRIPT

Don't worry that you can't give your kids the best of everything. Give them YOUR very best. H. Jackson Brown

The Loving Dictionary contains 1,001 esteeming adjectives. While there are numerous other adjectives that could have been included, I purposely chose to include the words that I believe to be the most affirming and positive.

I purposely chose to exclude two adjectives that, while generally perceived as having positive connotations, I believe could be more life-affirming. The two words are *hard-working* and *self-sacrificing.*

Hard-working, usually applied to men, and *self-sacrificing,* usually applied to women, have become more than adjectives. They have become ways of life that do not support living in balance and that rob us of the very joy of living.

To be diligent, industrious and successful does not mean that we have to work so hard that we drive our bodies, minds, hearts and souls to the breaking point. Nor does being generous, thoughtful and supportive mean that we need to sacrifice so much of our time and energy that we have nothing left over for ourselves.

All too frequently I hear the expressions *I'm so tired. I never have enough time.* Experience has taught me that what I'm really hearing is *I'm so tired of not living, of not having enough time and energy for myself, for just being.*

Lack of time and energy is the result of not saying NO, of not setting respectful limitations on our time, energy and resources. It's the biggest issue that gets addressed in my *Boundaries Program* where people learn how to set limits and say NO.

Many people don't even realize that they have the right to say NO. They need permission because saying NO can bring up a lot of fear for them—fear of not being liked, of hurting another person's feelings, of abandonment, of being fired or losing business.

For others, the issue is not knowing *how* to say NO. Without the ability to set healthy boundaries, we can sacrifice our time and life energy to the point of depression, sickness and poverty. Not the poverty of money, rather the poverty of spirit, joy and hope.

In reality, when we choose to create quality time for ourselves and for our loved ones, we send a powerful message of respect to everyone around us. Contrary to popular belief, that message is like a beacon that draws even more respect, love and success. When we come to life refreshed and happy, life responds in kind.

I support you in substituting more life-affirming words for these two adjectives. Of course, if they have a very positive meaning *for you*, then please continue to use them. Words can mean so many different things to different people. First and foremost, I support you in trusting what's right *for you.*

BIBLIOGRAPHY

Canfield, Jack. *Self-Esteem and Peak Performance.* Boston, Allyn & Bacon, 1995.

Chapman, Gary. *The Five Love Languages.* Chicago, Northfield Publishing, 1995.

Chopra, Deepak. *Ageless Body, Timeless Mind.* New York, Harmony Books, 1993.

Clance, Pauline Rose. *The Impostor Phenomenon: Overcoming the Fear That Haunts Your Success.* Atlanta:, Peachtree Publishers, Ltd., 1985.

Cloud, Henry and Townsend, John. *Boundaries, When to Say "Yes" When to Say "No".* Michigan, Zondervan Publishing House, 1995.

Covey, Stephen R. *The Seven Habits of Highly Effective People.* New York, Fireside, 1989.

Helmstetter, Shad. *The Self-Talk Solution.* New York, POCKET BOOKS, 1987.

Helmstetter, Shad. *How To Excel In Times of Change.* New York, POCKET BOOKS, 1991.

Jeffers, Susan. *Feel The Fear And Do It Anyway.* New York, Fawcett Columbine, 1987.

Rosenberg, Marshall B. *Non-Violent Communication, A Language of Compassion.* California, PuddleDancer Press, 1999.

Sher, Barbara. *Wishcraft, How To Get What You Really Want.* New York, Ballantine Books, 1979.

Walther, George R. *Power Talking.* New York, Berkley Publishing Group, 1992.

Ziglar, Zig. *Raising Positive Kids in a Negative World.* New York, Ballantine Books, 1989.

HOW TO CONTACT

For information on Marian York and how to bring WORDpower™ keynotes and training programs to your company, association, school or event visit:
www.mywordpower.com

Or contact:

Marian York
206-526-5223

The WORDpower™ Institute NW
7552 12th Avenue NE
Seattle, WA 98115
Email: speaker@mywordpower.com
Fax: 206-523-9204

HOW TO ORDER

WORDpower™ For Success And Change!
Now Available On Audio Tape

With Marian York

WORDpower™ 101 - Three Hours Of WORDpower™ Basics

- Discover The Science of WORDpower™
- Explore FAB...Feelings, Attitudes And Beliefs
- Utilize The WORDpower™ Arm Exercise
- Learn The 3 Key WORDpower™ Expressions
- Change Limiting Beliefs With Bridge Language
- Bust Through Procrastination With Baby Steps
- Increase Productivity With Proactive WORDpower™

$29.99

To Order Visit www.mywordpower.com

Or Send Check Payable To:

WORDpower™ Institute NW
7552 12th Avenue NE
Seattle WA 98115
206 526-5223

PLEASE PRINT
Name______________________________
Street Address______________________________
City, State, Zip______________________________
Phone With Area Code______________________________
Payment Visa/MC ______________________Exp. Date________
Name on Card ________________Signature________________

Quantity WORDpower™ Audio Series	$29.99 Per Set	WA Residents Only Add 8.6% Tax	$3.00 Shipping & Handling Add $1.50 Per Additional Item	TOTAL Amount O[f] Order

(Outside US add $6.00. For orders outside of US, please pay in US dollars only.)

ABOUT THE AUTHOR

An authority on proactive communication skills, Marian York is the creator of Proactive *WORDpower™ - The Language of Leadership.* A national speaker and trainer, she is highly sought after by national associations and corporations to present motivational and educational programs on such diverse issues as performance, change, effective communication, quality of life and building relationships of trust. Founder of the WORDpower™ Institute NW, Marian is the author of *The Loving Dictionary* and the popular *WORDpower™ For Success And Change* audio series. Her greatest accomplishment to date is being able to look at herself in the mirror and appreciate who she sees. Marian lives in Seattle, Washington.